IRREVERENCE
A Strategy for Therapists' Survival

Other titles in the
Systemic Thinking and Practice Series
edited by David Campbell & Ros Draper
published and distributed by Karnac Books

IRREVERENCE
A Strategy
for Therapists' Survival

Gianfranco Cecchin, M.D.
Gerry Lane, M.S.W.
Wendel A. Ray, Ph.D.

Foreword by
Bradford P. Keeney, Ph.D.
Professor and Director of Scholarly Studies,
University of St. Thomas, St. Paul, Minnesota

Systemic Thinking and Practice Series

Series Editors
David Campbell & Ros Draper

Karnac Books
London **1992** New York

First published in 1992 by
H. Karnac (Books) Ltd.
58 Gloucester Road,
London SW7 4QY

Distributed in the United States of America by
Brunner/Mazel, Inc.
19 Union Square West
New York, NY 10003

ISBN 1 85575 031 7

Printed in Great Britain by BPCC Wheatons Ltd, Exeter

CONTENTS

EDITORS' FOREWORD

The process of creating this book began when the three authors sat down to share their thinking about some of their more difficult cases. They discovered they had similar views, their discussion was fruitful, and they agreed to carry on the conversation the next time their paths crossed. They met several more times, and found their shared ideas began to coalesce around a concept they called "irreverence". However, these clinicians do not work together, they do not belong to the same research project, and they are separated by thousands of miles. Instead they were joined by a similar openness to new ideas, and they were able to influence and be influenced by each other in such a way that this innovative thinking has become clarified for all to understand and put to use. As editors we have been delighted to be part of this process and to be able to bring this book to the reader.

This book is not a rationale for collecting different techniques for use in difficult situations. Rather, it is an affirmation that systemic therapists must always be on the edge, open to new ways of seeing things and new ways of intervening; they must always be prepared to say, "Yes, but there is another way to see this". This ability lies at the heart of systemic practice, and these authors have found a way of helping therapists stay on the edge with even the most difficult cases.

We hope the reader will think of "irreverence" as the milestone in the progression of systemic ideas that have emerged from the fertile minds of the original Milan group. We see "irreverence" as a development of the concept of "curiosity" which was a development of the concept of "neutrality" before that.

The family therapy field is also developing, and we see therapists breaking down many of the traditional boundaries associated with "schools of therapy". The contexts in which family work is done seem increasingly complex as issues such as child protection, gender, and race, are given greater prominence. Therapists are developing new models that span the boundaries which seemed inviolate a few years ago. This book offers the reader a systemic framework from which to challenge the current ideologies, whether they be in the family or in the field, or in the mind of the therapist.

David Campbell
Ros Draper

London

FOREWORD

Bradford P. Keeney

During medieval times a holiday took place throughout Europe called the Feast of Fools. Although not popular with the nobility and ruling class, it was celebrated by the locals, who, dressed up as church and court officials, ridiculed and rendered absurd the most respected ideas, ideals, rituals, and customs.

An important contribution of the Feast of Fools was to disempower the powerful and empower the local citizenry. As Harvey Cox (1969, p. 5) notes, "unmasking the pretence of the powerful always makes the power seem less irresistible", and this "is why tyrants tremble before fools and dictators ban political cabarets".

In this present volume, an odd custom has re-entered our ranks to celebrate a feast of irreverence. In doing so, everyday practitioners may be freed from the irresistible grip of professional schools, journals, books, master therapists, and all the pomp and regalia of the field.

More than a release from the received and chained views of pious professionalism, the contribution of Cecchin, Lane, and

Ray is an invitation to play and take play seriously to make serious contributions to the lives of clients. Through the practice of irreverence, we will sometimes fail to honour, venerate, or even practise the axioms set forth by the various psychotheologies. Our work will instead be more organized by curiosity, desire, passion, imagination, invention, creativity, and improvization.

The reverent therapist is one committed to revering *relevance*, no matter how irreverent his conduct may be in order to achieve it. This relevance is respectful of "difference" as well as "absence" in the lives of clients, therapists, and the social institutions embodying them. Stated differently, the "difference that makes a difference" is as revered as the absence that makes an "absence". Trying to deconstruct, evaporate, withdraw, or ignore so-called pathologizing is often as valuable as constructing tangible resources for therapeutic change.

The authors are to be applauded for accepting and rejecting all totalizing theories and practices of therapies. They show that every sacred cow in the field is sacred for only a moment, for the holy therapeutic breath always moves on to embrace the next contribution in the ever-lasting conversation making up the history of the profession. Every particular understanding stands under the subsequent one, although it may differ and sometimes even seem to negate it. Seen in this more global and ecological way, the revered "truths" of practice are not solidified commandments in stone, but flexible benchmarks, partly relevant and partly irrelevant. Their "realness" is about as fixed and solid as a sugar-cube buoy floating on a restless sea.

Readers approaching the buoy thrown out by Cecchin, Lane, and Ray should take notice of their own responses to it. Does it evoke freedom, play, imagination, and irreverence? More specifically, do you find yourself being irreverent to it? If so, the authors have succeeded in getting you to dance with them.

If not, then I suggest you have taken the book too seriously. You have approached the book, and perhaps the context of the whole field in which it is a part, with too much reverence. For such readers, an intervention may be suggested:

Open the book randomly to any page and point your finger to any sentence or paragraph. Write a counter paragraph stating why you believe no one should be irreverent to the subject matter the sentence(s) address. Then write a letter to the authors thanking them for inspiring you to write the specific counter paragraph. Make certain you say this with finely polished irreverence, so they can taste their own medicine!"

I welcome all clinicians to this feast of fools. The celebration juggles the entire field and offers one transformation after another of practitioners' eternal verities. The occasion is one of dancing in the streets and turning everything upside down and inside out. When the feast is over, we can go back to our jobs with revitalized reverence for irreverence and a further affirmation of being human.

PREFACE

W e come from very different experiences; we are of different ages and backgrounds. For a number of years each of us has separately been pursuing our work in systemic family therapy in different parts of the world. After several chance meetings at different workshops, we found ourselves in an intense, on-going conversation about such topics as strategizing, cybernetics (first and second order), and narrative in relation to our practice. From these meetings an organizing theme emerged that we eventually decided to call *irreverence*. Over the course of the subsequent two years we have been meeting regularly in Atlanta, Georgia, for the purpose of elaborating this idea of irreverence.

In writing this book, it is our hope to offer to the readers a meta-perspective that holds the potential for lifting some people out of what we experience as an endless debate about such dichotomies as strategizing versus non-intervention, power versus respect, narrative versus cybernetics, and about which school of therapy is "more correct". This book is our contribution to this lively debate. We invite the reader to join our conversation.

ACKNOWLEDGEMENTS

The authors would like to thank Tom Corbett and Charlie Tauber of Hillside Hospital, Atlanta, Georgia, for their kind support of this project.

AUTHORS' NOTE

Although the authors recognize the necessity for awareness of gender sensitivity, for the sake of simplicity the masculine pronoun has in general been used. Also, in the case examples that are used throughout the book to illustrate the authors' ideas, in order to maintain the highest level of confidentiality personal names—and if necessary the context of cases—have been altered or not presented.

CHAPTER ONE

The idea of irreverence

Some people are survivors, and others are annihilated by
life's tragedies, and that is just one of the cruelties of living.

Woody Allen

T his book is an attempt to describe our strategies for survival in the rough sea of family therapy. When you venture into these choppy waters, you are bound to meet
many dangers, whether you are a beginner or an expert.

As a beginner, the first problem you meet is to decide which
school to follow. Very soon you could be told that the school you
have chosen is part of your personal problems. Then, when you
begin to work in an institution, such as a psychiatric hospital,
you are told that, "Everything you learned in family therapy
training does not fit here". Searching for a life-line you go to
conferences where you meet gurus who convince you that they
have found the only right way to do therapy. When you try to
interview a couple or a family you either end up looking like

1

someone who has been brainwashed by the prevailing patriar-
chal culture, or make others uneasy by your politically correct
feminist leanings.

The most common double-bind you find yourself in is when a
supervisor or teacher tells you that everything you are doing is
wrong, too mechanical; it should be more spontaneously creative
(i.e. just like me). When you try to just talk to a family, the supervisor accuses you of being too conversational and not taking responsibility for change. If your behaviour is more directive and
solution-oriented, you are accused of becoming a dictator or
colonizer (Jackson, 1963) who does not respect the family story
enough.

To make things more complicated, there are still some people
who believe family therapy should become a hard science. And
what could be harder? As a therapist who is only doing his best
to help clients, you are told that your lack of success is due to not
having read enough research on family process. Usually you are
told something of that sort when your are in the middle of trying
hard to help a client solve a problem, and the last thing you need
to hear is this type of advice, which implies there is something
wrong with you for not being able to handle the family's problem on your own. Then they give you some sage advice, like,
"Why don't you make a genogram of your own family to find
out what is preventing you from being successful" (like me!).

As an expert therapist, in contrast, you are compelled to repeat
yourself, and, often you become addicted to your model. If you
are a teacher or a supervisor, your colleagues and students may
reinforce this tendency to become stuck, unable to consider other
ways of seeing the world. The people you teach or supervise feed
off and feed your certainty. When you feel you have created
some grand scheme for solving human suffering, you come into
contact with other professionals who are equally certain of the
correctness of their views. You are shocked to discover that they
have no faith in your vision and even belittle what they see as
your naive position.

If you dare to push your ideas beyond the safe boundaries of
the family therapy enclave, you may be astounded by how little
importance family therapy dogma has in the larger socio-politi-

cal world (courts, social welfare institutions, traditional psychiatry, etc.). For many years, for example, some of the most prestigious and influential leaders in the field of family therapy have attempted to implement well-thought-out systemic models in reforming the foster care programs in major cities around the world. Upon encountering the well-organized structure of such enormous bureaucracies, they have repeatedly discovered the limits of their prestige and ability to influence. Most of the time, the directors of these social welfare programs tell a would-be reformer that his ideas were theoretically interesting, especially to the workers at the direct service level. Unfortunately, however, the would-be reformers remain mystified as to why their ideas and techniques, which have proved very useful in working with an individual or with families, are not acceptable within such a well-established and multifaceted system as a large city welfare organization.

When, as an expert, you venture into publishing an important book or paper, some colleagues become loyal to your ideas and then insist that you stick with those original insights. Any move away from what people expect from you will be resented, or even denied. One frequently hears humorous stories about the profound meaning some people attached to any act of Milton Erickson during the last years of his life. If he fell asleep, it could be interpreted as a paradoxical signal for the person in his presence to relax (whereas it could simply have been that he was sleepy). The danger of becoming labelled as knowing a "truth" restricts both the "expert" and those who would learn from "experts". One of the authors, stuck with the reputation of being a paradoxical therapist, once forgot his role and, upon meeting a family, simply asked, "How are you?" One beginning student who was observing immediately turned to another and commented, "Where's the beef?"

In contrast to the trap where leaders are expected to maintain a stagnant position of "truth", Murray Bowen seemed to us to have been caught in an opposite position. Being one of the most important and influential seminal thinkers in the field, he spent a great deal of his energy trying to convince others of the scientific truth of his ideas, often showing frustration and irritation towards people who seemed unable or unwilling to understand his model. Not even the presence of a group of loyal followers seemed to diminish his annoyance at being misunderstood.

How then, as experts, can we survive between this Scylla and Charybdis of having people believe you so much that you become trapped, or of you believing so much in your own ideas that you spend all your time trying to guard the faith of your followers? Conversely, as beginners, how can you survive between the temptation to be a loyal student or becoming hopelessly eclectic? Perhaps one answer is to keep attending workshops and conferences, which seems to us to be necessary to sustain the illusion of the importance of family therapy in the world at large.

We, in some way, would like to recuperate the strengths of the family therapy movement, which has remained on the fringe of the culture and of the mental health field. The advantageous position of being on the fringe is a result of the near blasphemy of the originators of the family therapy field, who harshly challenged the prevailing psychiatric dogmas from the 1950s onward. Ironically, in our introducing the idea of irreverence in this book we consider ourselves to be quite conservative in our desire to recover this sense of intellectual freedom and integrity handed down to us by the originators of the field.

How did we arrive at the position of irreverence as an organizing principle for our survival? For many years each of us was plagued by doubts when we were learning, teaching therapy, sitting with a family, discussing with colleagues, and so forth. We were at war against our doubts, and we always felt we were losing because after brief victories these doubts would creep in again. This experience was demoralizing, as long as we considered it a handicap. Our belief at that time was that a responsible therapist should know and believe in what he is doing, without spending half his time brooding over it. Fortunately, after many years of frustration, we got fed up with it.

As is often the case for us when we reach such a demoralized state, we find the stories of Gregory Bateson to be helpful. In the 1960s Bateson was living in Hawaii, where he was involved in research on the communicative behaviour of porpoises. He worked with a group of young researchers who were also interested in studying the behaviour of dolphins, but who had very little money to support the research. So, they set up a program: they would train dolphins to do tricks and invite a public audience to pay a small admission fee to watch the dolphins perform. Being highly ethical, the group refused to show the porpoises repeating the same tricks over and over, because the idea was to allow the audience to watch the trainer teach them new tricks.

The story goes that one day they were working with a new dolphin. The trainer held a fish up, the dolphin jumped, and a fish was given. Later in the day the next audience came, the dolphin came around and performed the same trick, and, of course, the trainer did not reward him with a fish, because the idea was to perform a new trick. Eventually, after repeated failures to attain a fish because he kept repeating the same behaviour, the dolphin performed a new trick, a back-flip, and a fish was given to reward the new behaviour. Unfortunately, when the porpoise repeated the behaviour, it was not rewarded, even though the new trick was repeated several times. Right before the sixth performance, the trainers looked over at the holding tank and noticed that this dolphin was making an incredible amount of noise and splashing: the porpoise had performed six new tricks that had never before been recorded. Bateson's description of the situation was that through this long, frustrating process of repeating the same behaviour in hopes of getting a reward but being frustrated, the dolphin finally figured out that this was a situation in which new behaviour had to be demonstrated in order to gain a reward. The dolphin had learned how to learn.

Not unlike the dolphin in Bateson's famous story, we experienced a creative leap in learning. After years of frustration, we began to experience our doubting as a state of irreverence. Doubt became an asset rather than a hindrance.

In the chapters that follow, the reader will find different examples of therapeutic behaviour that we call irreverence. Many of the actions described will sound familiar, belonging to the paradoxical, strategic, and narrative models. We believe, however, that by using the word "irreverence" we compel ourselves to expand our reflections to encompass issues of pragmatics and ethics and even, if we are not too ambitious, to question the condition of being a human in this changing world.

For the past four or five years we have been fascinated by second-order cybernetics. This theory branched into two distinct directions. One, the theory of second-order cybernetics, emphasized the participation of the observer (therapist) in the system, as with Maturana and Varela's (1980) idea that it is impossible to have instructive interaction between living beings. Moreover, Von Foerster (1981) and Keeney (1982, 1983) proposed that relational reality is co-constructed in a linguistic domain. In addition, the work of Goldner (1988) and other feminist-oriented practitioners also challenges the limitations of first-order cybernetics in explaining the complexity of gender-related issues.

The second direction was a move completely away from the cybernetic metaphor, to that of a narrative epistemology. According to Anderson and Goolishian (1988, 1990), White (1989), and more recently Hoffman (1990), human beings are immersed in a narrative in which everyone participates, but which can create problems while simultaneously having the potential for dissolving them. Goolishian and Anderson advocate maintaining openness in the therapeutic conversation as a way of increasing the likelihood that multiple realities will emerge. One could characterize this movement towards non-instrumentality as a position of, "be careful, because if therapists give the illusion that they can do something, then the system will buy the illusion of power". In a sense these authors seem to say that to believe in power is to become an employee of social control, a dictator of what the therapist believes to be "healthy" or "normal" functioning.

In one sense the recent work of Goolishian and others was an antidote for those of us who had become overly infatuated with the concepts of strategizing and intervening. Goolishian, Hoffman, and Andersen's position on instrumentality was very important politically within the field. When therapy is based too much on the instrumentality of how to help people change, it runs the risk of becoming an instrument of the legal system. We consistently hear concern being voiced by therapists who fear that they are being placed in a position of becoming co-opted by the legal system, and therefore fear becoming stigmatized as social controllers.

An advantage of taking the position advocated by Goolishian is that one can avoid the trap of making promises to the family, the courts, and other institutions that one is able to help people change. We feel that therapists who make promises that they know how to communicate, or how to control, risk not only becoming dangerous to the clients but also being manipulated by agencies of social control.

Here is when the doubts that we mentioned earlier began to haunt us. It was in the moment when teachers and students began to ask questions like: If a client asks for help or a suggestion, why not respond? If a situation (e.g. abuse, violence, suicide) requires an authoritarian intervention, why not intervene? If someone looks for an "expert", why not offer one to him? If someone looks for a diagnostic label, why not give it to him as a solution? In essence, the question became: How can a systemic therapist recoup some initiative without falling into an already out-dated model based on the illusion of power and control?

To believe too much in non-instrumentality could result in one being trapped, restricted, and unable to act. One can become immobilized by the fear of being too active. Or, one could fall into the magic belief that changing narrative changes people. Many therapists are under the illusion that simply changing a label always solves even chronic family dramas. If a therapist is convinced that by giving up strategizing he can become effective, then he becomes a believer in the instrument of non-instrumentality. Often, the temptation to control through non-instrumentality comes back to haunt those of us who have gone through this process. Thus, the porpoise jump involves fighting the temptation ever to become a true believer in any one approach or theory (Whitaker, 1976).

In attempting to move to a position of irreverence, the question that must be asked is: Can this shift be made without falling back into the position of believing too much in our strategies or in the absence of strategies? One solution to this quandary is never to become completely seduced by one model or another. The irreverent therapist seeks never to feel the necessity to obey a

particular theory, the rules of the client, or the referral system—
i.e., the courts or social welfare agencies.

It is important to emphasize that it is useful to have clear in
your mind some ethical deontological principles that are part of a
lively debate today within the therapeutic community. [The term
"deontological" relates to "deontology", defined in *Webster's Unabridged Dictionary* (1983) as "that which is binding and proper", or,
more precisely, to "the theory of duty or moral obligation; ethics".]
The key premise is that excessive loyalty to a specific idea makes
the individual who embraces it irresponsible in relation to the
moral consequences inherently involved. If some disaster hap-
pens it is not the individual who is responsible, but the idea (with
a capital "I") from which the action springs (such as the position
taken by defendants at the Nuremberg Trials, for example, where
the claim was that they were not responsible for their behaviour
because of excessive loyalty to Third Reich). So, in the field of
psychiatry, a total commitment to the idea that mental disease is of
biological origin, or that the problem we face is a result of emotional or environmental deprivation, compels the therapist to become a manager of impossible situations. Then the only "ethical"
solution is to become an "expert" and "take charge" of the patient's
life.

From our viewpoint, which some may consider extreme, this
position is irresponsible because the therapist who takes this
stance often lacks the capacity to examine the pragmatic consequences of his own behaviour. He is not aware that his way of
acting and thinking has become part of the problem. Irreverence,
as described here, is an attempt to recoup what for us is a more
ethical deontological position.

Somebody could object: "If it is dangerous to believe too
strongly in a theory, then it would also seem useless to study or
conduct research—in therapy, anything goes." We would dis-
agree strongly with this. You have to know something very well
before you are able to be irreverent towards it. You should be
conversant with the literature of different therapeutic perspectives and be an "expert" in at least one of them. This is not to
say that even a beginning therapist cannot, under pressure from
either a supervisor or client, sense that what he is doing is not

working. Much more will be said about this point in chapter four, on training.

In summary, it is the therapist's enthusiasm for a model or a hypothesis that can help him to get close to a family, while simultaneously maintaining a certain level of curiosity and respect. But it is at the moment when the therapist begins to reflect upon the effect of his own attitude and presumptions that he acquires a position that is both ethical and therapeutic. In order to be able to attain this ability for self-reflexivity, we believe that it is necessary to have a certain level of irreverence and a sense of humour, which one acquires by maintaining a continuous conversation with colleagues, people outside the mental health field, students, and patients alike.

Irreverence varies greatly from being a revolutionary or from fighting oppression in the family and/or institution. It is a position reflective of a state of mind of the therapist that frees him by allowing him to take action without falling victim to the illusion of control. The position of systemic irreverence allows the therapist to juxtapose ideas that might at first look contradictory.

Furthermore, the irreverent therapist constantly undermines the patterns and stories constraining the family, promoting uncertainty, and thus allowing the client's system an opportunity to evolve new beliefs and meanings and less restrictive patterns. However, in moving towards a position of irreverence, the therapist attempts to remain free from the co-optive nature of consensual belief, to be willing not to become a true believer in what he is asked to do by the state, or the institution, or even the clinic in which he works.

A striking example can be seen in the behaviour of Fidel Castro as he attempts to adapt to the end of the cold war. This change appears to be having the effect of hardening Castro's belief in his own construction about what is the best form of government for Cuba. Even the slightest form of irreverence to his beliefs in communist doctrine must seem to him to be immoral. It appears that he is willing to bring Cuba and himself to the point of destruction in order to keep faith with the principles he has been loyal to for thirty years. To be disloyal to any part of his doctrine seems for Castro to be an unforgivable sin.

By becoming irreverent, the individual is free to be playful without falling into the impoverished meaning system that is constraining him. He is free to begin to look for the absurd aspects of the situation, as well as for the tragic.

In our small world of therapy, it is the irreverent therapist's job to undermine those aspects of the clients' reality that are restricting them from making the changes they desire. The irreverent therapist is sceptical towards polarities, thereby affording himself freedom from both the passive position of, "I must not go in and introduce an idea about how people can change," *and* the strategic position of, "I've got to come up with a tactic". With irreverence the therapist introduces an idea but does not necessarily believe that people should follow it.

Just as it is impossible not to communicate, it is also impossible not to have a hypothesis. Why should a therapist try to control a desire to formulate a hypothesis, an idea? Instead, why not utilize this notion to maximum benefit? As long as he does not fall in love with the hypothesis, as long as he plays with it, or talks to colleagues about it, there appears to be no valid argument to prevent him from building a hypothesis. The therapist can take responsibility for his feeling or guess, yet be willing to discard the idea when it is no longer useful. He can use hypotheses as descriptions rather than as explanations.

Sometimes the therapist may desire to take a more directive approach, such as performing a ritual. Why restrict oneself to being reverent to never doing anything? Why not sometimes take action? We postulate that it is appropriate to act as long as the therapist is willing to accept responsibility for his actions, particularly if he places a time-frame around the action he is taking. We want to emphasize this point. A therapist can easily say to a patient that he will consider him a psychiatric patient for the next two weeks during the patient's hospitalization. He can choose, temporarily, to control a patient's freedom during the time he believes the patient to be suicidal. He can take care of the life of an "incompetent" person for the time he believes that person to be incapable of taking care of himself. And lastly, as a student, he can choose to believe in a teacher during the two or four years that his training course lasts.

The therapist is not interested in knowing what really produces change, only in the change that actually occurs. Irreverence is to never accept one logical level of a position but, rather, to play with varying levels of abstractions, changing from one level to another. Instead of accepting any fixed descriptions, irreverence posits eroding certainty. Whenever the client expresses certainty, the irreverent therapist then describes the phenomenon at another level of abstraction. Such a position often involves doing the exact opposite of what received wisdom (Weakland, 1989) prescribes. The client came seeking change; however, the irreverent therapist may tell the client that what he is doing is good, go slow, don't change.

So, put your life-jacket on and get both oars into the water as we plunge into an irreverent excursion through the wonderfully perilous waters of family therapy.

CHAPTER TWO

Irreverence and violence

C ertain topics are so emotionally laden that some people seem to think that systemic ideas do not apply in such cases. Certain subjects or presenting problems are so sensitive that people have great difficulty moving beyond their own feelings. These problems include many kinds of interpersonal violence between genders, and particularly incest. It is almost as though where there are strong emotions, there is a strong tendency towards either/or dichotomization of the topic: black or white, good or bad, victim/victimized. In such instances individual perspectives become so reactive that it is difficult to believe that system theory applies, rather that it pertains only to very nice people. It is as though with certain topics only primitive responses prevail. Incest, child neglect or abuse, and spouse battering are examples of topics that evoke strong emotional reactions that can make effective therapy difficult.

One way of thinking about violence would be to consider the stories that are available today, in 1992. Victim and perpetrator, oppressor and oppressed, equal participation, impassioned and passionless—these are but a few. Two especially seem currently to prevail.

One, the feminist position, conceptualizes violence towards woman as being a product of women being victims of an oppressive male-dominated society. Feminists hold certain strong values about which they do not wish to be irreverent. For example, with respect to violence, the feminist position is very much like the more traditional orientations to violence (i.e. conceptualized in terms of a victim/victimizer duality). The second, the systemic orientation, moves away from the whole victim/victimizer dichotomy, choosing to focus more on the patterns of interaction that connect people and that trigger violent patterns of behaviour.

The irreverent perspective we are advocating allows the freedom to respect the values of both of these orientations without being restricted to absolute adherence to either one. Having too much faith in any position, any story, we run the risk of creating an inflexible, impoverished therapeutic reality. That is the essence of our irreverent position. We are not suggesting that irreverence is better than any other story. Rather, we pose the question, how can we train ourselves to be disloyal to *any* story when or if it becomes no longer useful?

Without seeming disrespectful to the potential dangers of the world, we would like to echo a provocative point of view voiced by Camile Paglia, who makes a strong case in her book *Sexual Persona* (1989) that there are situations in which it is too simple to think that violence towards women is a political problem of power. Paglia is of the opinion that sex can be a far darker power for both men and woman than has generally been admitted. Sex and violence have been part of our human history for centuries—they are nothing new. Society, according to Paglia, was created by humans to defend us from nature—but nature keeps seeping in, in millions of ways.

Society is an artificial construction. A defense against nature's power. Without society, we would be a storm tossed on a barbarous sea that is nature. Society is a system of inherent form reducing our humiliating passivity to nature. We may alter these forms slowly or suddenly, but no change in society will ever change nature. [p. 4]

Even though as therapists we persistently strive to eliminate these aspects of human behaviour, violence, rape, and incest are always with us. As therapists, when we encounter these situations, we should not be so paralysed. Such events are natural phenomena, so why be terrified? When we react purely emotionally, it becomes our problem and we are then of little help to our clients. Paglia does not condone violence; rather, she acknowledges its existence as part of nature. In a post-modern world where many of the certainties that acted to separate us from nature, and upon which we have relied so heavily, are now being questioned, it is essential, according to Paglia, to remember that we are a part of and are immersed in nature.

Paglia (1989) also challenges the radical feminist notion that women are the victims of men:

Male bonding and patriarchy were the recourse to which man was forced by his terrible sense of woman's power, her imperviousness, her archetypal confederacy with chthonian nature. Woman's body is a labyrinth in which man is lost. It is a walled garden, a medieval hortus conclusus, in which nature works its daemonic sorcery. Woman is the primeval fabricator, the real first mover. She turns a gob of refuse into a spreading web of sentient being, floating on the snaky umbilical by which she leashes every man. [p. 12]

A contrast to both the feminist's and Paglia's stories is the systemic orientation, which, rather than placing primary emphasis on the individual, is more concerned with the circular nature of causality, feedback, pattern, and the relationships between people. Any of these theories can be useful in a given situation. As therapists we are there to assist, so we should use whatever stories are contextually appropriate in helping the clients.

As therapists with a particular love for a systemic orientation, one observation that we have found useful is that in many cases involving violence, there is a strong undercurrent of sexual passion—a prevailing theme that we encountered during the course of working with many court-referred violent families. We be-

came interested in the idea that in many instances passion somehow holds couples together, even though there is severe violence
in the relationship. What we have found is that the so-called
sado-masochistic aspect can be very sexy, very passionate, and
extremely dangerous for many of these couples. We have found
this to be a particularly resourceful story to examine when working with couples' violence.

In our experience, even though we often observed passion
as an important part of many violent situations, we have been
somewhat reticent about starting to talk about this with other
colleagues in the field, because we feared attack by the feminists
for not recognizing that women are oppressed. Now, one of
the things that seems to disturb some therapists the most about
working with violence is that they cannot stand both the intense
level of physical pain and the sexual passion present within a
couple. Couples involved in violence are often extremely intense
about each other, and frankly many therapists with conventional
middle-class values are afraid to think about violence from a
non-traditional perspective—for example, as being a matter of
passion that leads to a violent dance in which two adults are
involved—let alone actually to do anything controversial when
working with violence.

In many instances, couples involved in violence are willing to
die for those relationships, willing to die for the passion, willing
to risk their lives. Some therapists have difficulty understanding
this since they, themselves, would rather divorce—just pay the
legal fees and go. This seems to us to be a commonly held west-
ern cultural pattern.

Recognizing that a therapist can be organized by any one of a
number of different stories, the question then becomes, what do
you do? Every therapist, of course, chooses one story or another.
It is impossible not to choose. If you are a feminist, you are organized by the feminist bias. If you are a cybernetically oriented
therapist you are organized by a systemic bias—Bowen, MRI,
solution-focused, Milan, etc. The therapist chooses the one he
feels most comfortable with. In contrast, the irreverent therapist
is willing to abandon his prejudice if he is stuck, and to choose
another that better fits the clinical situation. Our point is that

therapists should strive to be aware of the consequences of the choices they make. This is the responsible position therapeutically.

The homicidal lady and the polite therapist

A violent couple came for treatment after the husband had, on two occasions, been physically violent with the wife. The wife had responded by fighting back, attacking him as well. Based on the interviews, the therapist was convinced that the man was involved in a gay relationship with another man. The therapist was worried that the husband would spread AIDS to the wife. She was a victim. The therapist felt very protective towards this wife and formed a very strong attachment to her. He attempted to separate the couple, suggesting that the woman leave her husband and go to a shelter for battered women. The therapist took a traditional victim/victimizer position, insisting that the husband was an oppressor who was victimizing his wife.

One of the authors was called in as a consultant in the aftermath of the case: the woman had murdered her husband after an argument during which the husband had announced he was leaving to go to live with his gay lover. At the time of the consultation, even though the woman had killed the husband, the therapist still continued to view the woman as the victim of the man.

What can be learned from a tragic case like this? It looked as though the therapist, by taking an inflexible victim/victimizer position, was unable to help the couple to disengage from their deadly dance. He was so reverent to the idea of victim and oppressor that through his inability to help the couple generate alternative premises and patterns he participated in creating a context in which the wife killed her husband. By being so loyal to the ideas of victim/victimizer, the therapist helped to set up a therapeutic context in which there was no possibility for change. One could say that the process of joining with the wife by continually emphasizing that the husband was oppressing her, contributed to the wife developing an inability to see any option other than murder.

One really sad aspect of this story is that some people—including many therapists—would say, "See, we knew this was going to lead to violence". If the therapist continues to maintain that in situations in which men oppress women such things happen, he can then walk away feeling validated about the seriousness of the situation, voicing such justifications as: "I knew all along that this was a very dangerous situation. If I could only have gotten the man to stop oppressing her, she wouldn't have been pushed to the point of killing him." And the therapist would never even recognize that he had participated in some way in setting the scenario such that deadly violence would occur.

The supervisor in this case was also partially responsible, in that he was unable to convince the therapist to loosen up. The supervisor tried to discourage the therapist's hard-line oppressor/oppressed position, but became so annoyed about this inflexible feminist position that he took the opposite pole and became fanatically anti-feminist. Becoming too rigidly anti-feminist, the supervisor enflamed the therapist's feminist orientation. As long as the supervisor rejected the therapists' position that the husband was oppressing the wife, the therapist could not hear the supervisor. The supervisor was not able to talk effectively to the therapist who, in turn, was not able to see the situation differently—and so the tragedy happened. Why was the supervisor unable to convince the therapist? Because he was so fanatical about his own idea that he created a symmetrical escalation from which neither of them could escape.

The therapist had a terrible emotional reaction to the tragedy. Later, but too late, he started to think about the implications of holding on adamantly to an oppressor/victim framework. When you think about therapeutic responsibility, consider the potential danger of believing too strongly in your paradigm. What is the point?

The passionless couple

In another instance, a case referred through the courts involved a man who was a pianist in a jazz band. He and his wife came to therapy because his wife had beaten him up. She was very violent with him, pushing him around because he drank and watched television all the time. The daughters aligned with the mother, and they all criticized him for the drinking, for watching too much television, for not doing enough work around the house. Eventually what happened through the therapeutic conversation over time is that the wife—an executive with a very good job—got so fed up with him that she kicked him out. He got his own place and ended up surviving, and the family also survived. He still had a poor relationship with his children after that.

It was a very simple story, with no magic solution, but it demonstrates a slightly different slant on couples' violence. The woman was not oppressing the man, but bullying him and beating him up. The wife realized that the husband was not going to change. He was not going to become involved with her, he was not going to become more responsible around the house. The husband became more aware that he really was not interested in this family. He was much more interested in television and music, and he preferred being alone. So, through the therapeutic conversation, they realized that there was really no reason to stay together.

The wife took the initiative to ask him to leave, and the violence stopped. She had been so frustrated with him that she would attack him and start hitting him, punching him. He would then call the police. What therapy did was help each of them decide that what they were doing together was not useful. They were not having their needs met.

How does this example reflect an irreverent position? With this family, the therapist was working on the basis of the hypothesis that violence always involves passion, that violence is a sign of passion. For months the therapist tried to bring out the passion, the bond, but then it just was not helpful. The couple kept repeating themselves. Nothing changed. Then the therapist happened to wake up one morning with the idea that he had to be disloyal to his hypothesis and adopt a different one because they couple just did not like each other. The therapist finally had to say, "Hey, there is no passion here". With the other couples he was working with, the passion that connected them was clear, but this one did not make sense.

For us, the interesting aspect of this case was the therapist's initial conviction that where there is violence there is always passion. In therapy, the story shifted to talking so much about passion that the couple realized that there was no passion remaining between them. Searching for the passion was helpful; but then the therapist came to the realization that he had to be disloyal to his idea that such couples are always very passionate. He was then free to ask himself if there was another possibility. Interestingly enough, once the therapist had come to this conclusion he discovered during the next session that both spouses were having similar ideas. In therapy they began to talk about, "Why don't you just end this? Why not just leave?" Was the therapist the one to suggest that the passion was gone, or was it the clients? Who knows.

By talking about passion, they became aware that they did not have any. The couple finally got so fed up with coming and trying to find how to shift the passion of violence to more affection and love that they decided they did not really want to be together. But they were only able to do this after the therapist had awoken to the idea that his passion for the passion theory was no longer useful. His irreverence to his own idea was helpful to the couple in deciding to separate.

How was the therapist able to abandon a theory that had previously been useful in working with so many couples with violence? He became totally frustrated and said to himself, "I can't figure out why you continue to stay together. I cannot find the connection, the passion here. All I find is frustration, hatred." The therapist's irreverence to his own conceptualization of the situation as being passion became the healthy moment of the therapy. His ability to question his own way of looking at the situation helped the couple to make a move. The therapy became unstuck the moment the therapist began to have doubts about his own theory. When one is able to doubt one's own theory, the client is given permission to move.

To reiterate, a key for accessing irreverence is for the therapist to have the courage to recognize the source of his frustration and take action in questioning his own theory about the situation, instead of being protective of himself. That is the art of becoming irreverent. One could say that when the therapist starts getting frustrated, it is a symptom or a sign that he may have become too reverent to his own story. Which means also that one should not be afraid to be irreverent. A part of being irreverent, is to have the courage to *not* fight for an idea that is no longer useful or congruent to the context at hand. This is a healthy thing you can do for your sanity, as well as for the client.

The nowhere man

A colleague came for a consultation, bringing a story about a patient that was very upsetting for him. He had been working with a 40-year-old chronic patient who had been a heavy utilizer of psychiatric and social services, going to the out-patient clinic for medication, and otherwise living a life of isolation from others. The therapist became very fascinated by the patient and set out to help him become a more socially active person. He devised a programme of treatment for the patient. In a very gentle manner, he organized group interactions for him and helped him get into an apartment for mental patients, where he could work with other people in learning basic living skills such as cooking and so forth. The patient struggled with these changes at first but seemed eager to please the therapist, and he followed the programme of treatment. To the therapist the patient seemed to improve. He was gradually becoming more social with other people in the apartment complex, participating more actively in group activities, and was even at the point of attaining a job. Just when it appeared that the patient was making noticeable improvement, the therapist received news that the patient had hung himself during a trip to a distant city to visit his family. The therapist was shocked. He could not understand what had happened. In the supervision group discussion a hypothesis emerged, which posited, "Is it possible that, faced with the challenge of finding a job and more intense involvement with other people, the patient had an experience of *lower* self-esteem because of an increased awareness of his inability to really get touch with other people?" Did the therapist's efforts to help him have the opposite effect, that of pushing him towards suicide?

From our point of view, the patient was not able to be irreverent to the therapist's attempts to help him, and the therapist was unable to be disloyal to the theory that human beings are more healthy if they socialize. It is also possible that the patient was unable to be irreverent to his family's need for him to have problems. He may have preferred to kill himself—and be institutionalized, through death, as unsuccessful—rather than risk improvement. The therapist, however, was a traditionally trained psychiatrist whose training did not involve consideration of the family situation.

The therapist who became the father

Another case involved multiple suicide attempts on the part of an 18-year-old daughter and later by her mother. Therapy seemed to be progressing well when the therapist realized he had been seeing the family for over six months—which is an unusually long period of treatment in this work setting. What finally dawned on the therapist was that the therapy was stuck because he kept trying to do the same thing with the husband and wife that they, as parents, were attempting to do with their daughter. The therapist was attempting to make them change how they were behaving with one another. In a way he was attempting to coerce them to change, and in so doing was instigating the very behaviour he was trying to help them change. It was the therapist's addiction to his idea about how the couple should act and his subsequent stubborn demand that they conform to his viewpoint, and not that of the family, that was keeping things stuck. Having finally realized that he was paralleling the same process that the parents were doing with their daughter, he pulled back, changing his own conceptual frame and how he was behaving towards the family. Immediately the tension broke between the husband and wife. The father was able to loosen up in his demands towards the daughter to grow up according to his plan. The mother and father began renegotiating their relationship, beginning to adjust to life with one another after the children had left the home. It was only after the therapist was able to challenge his own beliefs about what was wrong with the family, after he began to act differently towards them, that the family began to improve.

What, then, is irreverent about this case? The irreverence occurred when the therapist realized that his conceptualization and attempt to control the parents' style of parenting was similar to the way in which the father was trying to control the daughter and wife. This realization came to the therapist like a slap in the face . Therapy started progressing only after the therapist became irreverent to his own hypothesis.

Punishment as treatment

In a consultation group a female therapist described a case from a sex-offenders group she was leading. The group was made up of men who had sexually abused children. Many of the men had served time in prison for this crime. Some had been given the option to attend the group in order to avoid longer prison sentences; for others, involvement in the group was a condition of parole. This particular group had been on-going for several years.

The dilemma that the therapist brought to the group was that a man who had been a loyal member of the group for some time, one who, the therapist believed, had stopped any type of sexual abuse, was arrested, accused of molesting his 3½-year-old granddaughter. The therapist was shocked and angry about the recurrence of sexual abuse, appearing to view it as a personal affront.

The therapist related that over the course of treatment she was certain that the man had made progress, and she could not fathom the idea that he would go back to this behaviour. She was angry at him and felt he deserved to be punished for the crime.

She also noticed that the other men in the group were very anxious about the revelation, since members had great difficulty even admitting that they had sexual desires for children.

The therapist conveyed that her original contract with the group members was that if they were involved again in any child molestation, they would not be allowed to continue in the group. However, the man was denying the accusation that he had sexually abused his granddaughter, even though his daughter-in-law (the child's mother) had taken the child to the police and reported the story.

From a family perspective, the daughter-in-law had also accused the man of raping her several years earlier. He had also denied that charge and, subsequently, no action had been taken by the police. Interestingly enough, the daughter-in-law had sent her 3½-year-old child to spend the night with the grandparents. The child had slept in the bed with both grandparents, and it was during this time that she was allegedly molested by the grandfather.

The consultation group was struck by the possibility that the daughter-in-law may have sent her daughter to spend the night at the grandparents' house in order to set up her father-in-law, as an act of revenge for her past rape. As stated above, he denied all accusations.

The therapist was stuck as to how this information should be used in the sexual-offenders group. One suggestion was that she could tell the man in front of the group that over the course of the preceding year and a half he had convinced her that she had cured him of his paedophile tendencies. Another idea involved the fact that the men in the sexual-offenders group always denied that they experienced these paedophile feelings. This man had allegedly acted on some feeling that could result in a long prison term. He had carelessly allowed himself to sleep in the same bed with his granddaughter. We recommended that the therapist state to the group that sexual impulses are extremely powerful; one can be lulled into thinking that this behaviour is under control, and then a tragedy like this can take place. It is unfortunate that the man has to face the consequences of this accusation; however, for the group it is a helpful reminder to everyone of the danger involved in allowing themselves to be placed in such vulnerable situations.

In the consultation group the question arose as to whether kicking the man out of the treatment group would be helpful to the group as a whole. If he was allowed to remain, would it damage the contract and premise held within the group that members could remain only as long as they did not sexually abuse children? The solution to this dilemma suggested by the consultation group was for the man to be temporarily suspended from the group during the investigation and possible trial. If found innocent of the charges, he could return.

It appeared to the consultant that over time the therapist had become a true believer in the power of this sexual-molestation group process to cure paedophilic behaviour. This experience challenged the therapist's certainty about the absolute curative value of the group process. Later the therapist expressed that she felt relieved of a burden of responsibility she had been carrying for preventing future sexual misbehaviour by the group members. The therapist was able to become more flexible, better able to have a meaningful therapeutic relationship with the group members, by being able to facilitate a more open conversation about the very forbidden topics for which they were there to begin with. She felt she would be able to use this ability to acknowledge doubt to the treatment group about the power of the group process to cure the desires to have sexual relations with children. The group members could, however, support one another and provide a context in which they could safely discuss these taboo desires, providing a context in which they could express their fears and concerns.

With the idea of irreverence we emphasize the importance of therapeutic responsibility. What kind of story do you, as a therapist, prefer? When you prefer one story, are you able, if you see problems coming up, to be disloyal to your own stories when they are no longer useful? Can you dare to consider being irreverent to what you "know" is "the" correct way of thinking, at times when it is not useful? Any story—any of the current ways of thinking about a given situation—if you are too loyal to it, can create problems. This is an essential aspect of the final example.

A midsummer night's dream

Another example of work with violence involved a couple. The man was very violent, with a history of beating the woman frequently and severely . Her two teenage daughters from a previous marriage could not tolerate this man and refused to accept him as part of the family. They kept complaining to the mother, "Why do you keep him?", while at the same time they were misbehaving to such an extent that therapy was recommended by the school.

An important issue that came up at the beginning of therapy was that the mother insisted that her boyfriend behave like a father to her daughters, but the daughters continued to see him merely as an unworthy mate of their mother. The girls were furious at any attempt of the man to be a father to them. They did not want to come to therapy. The mother, in contrast, wanted to, in the hope that it would help her daughters accept her man and that by this acceptance he would beat her less.

After the second session the daughters became annoyed and dropped out of therapy. A hypothesis was made that as the man liked to come to therapy and that since therapy had begun his behaviour had improved slightly, the danger for the daughters was that he was becoming more acceptable to their mother, who, they feared, would become even more reluctant to kick him out. Therapy continued with the couple alone. The man described how he was furious with his girlfriend much of the time, complaining of her coldness and distance. He said he did not want to beat her, but she provoked him with her aloofness. When the conversation turned to his family of origin, a complex story emerged, related to his psychotic sister, who was still living with their violent father. The man described his father as being a brilliant man who controlled his family with an iron fist.

The man felt his family did not understand him and he was furious about it. He perceived himself to be in a weak position, which triggered angry outbursts. When he tried to explain himself, he felt no one would listen. In this new relationship he saw himself as being in a position that was very similar to the one he had in his father's family, one where no one ever took him seriously.

After several therapeutic conversations, some remarks seemed to have a particular effect on him. It was when the therapist asked, "Why do you take her so seriously? Everything she does, you think she's thinking about you? You think everything she does is a message to you. Why do you have this crazy idea? Perhaps she is thinking about somebody else, her mother, her sister, her daughter. She cannot be thinking only about you all the time. You keep saying that you are not important. So why should she think of you all of the time?"

The man came back to the next session, saying that that idea had had a great effect on him, and he felt he was less angry. The fact that he began to see his woman as someone who is not always trying to give a message to him was a great relief for him. He also mentioned some improvement in his relationship with his family of origin. The woman kept silent throughout most of this conversation.

At the next session the woman began the conversation in a very decisive tone, saying to the therapist before he had a chance to talk: "First this man was beating me up all the time and I had to take it. I couldn't get out because it was like an addiction. I wanted to get out, but I couldn't. Then I came into therapy, and the therapy has been good for him, right? And I have to come here to get all these insults during these meetings. I have to sit here and listen to all this bullshit conversation just for him to feel good. First I was abused because he had to take all the problems he has with his mother and father out on me by beating me. Then, he uses me to get therapy so he can feel better. He needed therapy to get better and he is doing fine, but what about me? What do I get out of this?"

The therapist naively commented that her boyfriend had stopped beating her. To which she responded "I don't believe in this systemic therapy, where people are seen as co-responsible for his violence—He is responsible! He is the only one responsible! You should punish him, not me! I'm furious that I decided to come to therapy and he is the one who is getting better. I am being punished, and he should have been punished for beating me! I'm mad! I'm mad at you!"

The woman's anger and request for punishment for her boyfriend took the therapist by surprise and upset him. The therapist said, "I have to think about this. What you are saying is a shock to me". The therapist left the room to talk with the team. The team felt that they had misunderstood the woman's initial request in therapy and that the hypothesis that the beating was part of a communication did not fit.

The therapist rejoined the couple with no specific idea about what to do. The woman continued her complaint: "We are still together, but I feel damaged. Also, now that the violence has stopped, I find him boring and superficial, and yet I feel compelled to stay with this goddamned, pig, bastard. I want him punished. You helped him feel better without punishing him, and I am furious. Two men here getting together, he's getting better and he doesn't even get any punishment. He got away with it. So what do you do now? I don't like it!"

The therapist ended the session with these words: "Look, you're perfectly right. It will take me time to think because I have this orientation in my head that says that not beating is better than beating, and that punishing is not helpful. Now you tell me that to get away with crime without punishment is not a solution. I don't know what to do. I should do something, but it is going to take me time to think about this. We will discuss it further at the next session."

At the next session he started talking about punishment. What kind of punishment does she think he should be given? How long should the punishment last? Weeks? Months? Years? A life time? "It looks like your daughters are doing a lot of punishing now by mistreating him!"

At this moment in therapy the therapist had changed the conversation from content (the punishment) to the process (the need to punish in order to maintain the relationship). But in his heart the therapist did not change his position from thinking that to cooperate and be gentle with each other was still a better solution.

In ending the session, the therapist stated: "I will not see you for six months because of an illness. My sickness is that I think cooperation is better than fighting; that's my prejudice. So we should keep away from each other for a while. You go on mistreating him. For me, the fact that there is no physical violence is already progress. But you have demonstrated to me that revenge is what is important in life. I need time to cure myself of my prejudice."

The clients came back six months later looking better. The woman was a little angry and was talking more during the session. She began by saying, "I'm doing okay since I've asked my boyfriend to leave home". (Since he moved out, they were visiting each other two to three times a week.) The man sat quietly and was very polite. They then told a story about a visit they had made to their relatives in a small village in Italy. They described numerous stories about aunts and uncles spending an inordinate amount of time conniving intricate plots for revenging new and past slights and wrong-doings.

This was illuminating for the therapist. He realized that he had not taken into account the larger culture. He realized that his prejudice made it impossible for him to see that revenge and vindictiveness is an important part of some cultures. What the therapist discovered was that he was not talking the language of the culture. The therapist was part of a therapeutic culture that places greater value on cooperation than on war. He told the couple about his discovery, describing with much emotion this new insight, speaking without interruption for more than ten minutes. Finally the couple gave in and began to laugh at the absurdity of the therapist's rambling, saying, "O.K., O.K., let's forget about this for now" and asked permission to leave early. As they were going out, the wife, in a playful way, said: "We will call you in a few months to see how you are doing."

Six months later the couple telephoned and asked for another session. When they came in, they appeared healthy and well groomed. The man had lost some weight, and the wife appeared to be four or five months pregnant. They looked like a couple waking up from a long midsummer night's dream. They said they were back together, and that her daughters had decided to stay with them and were looking forward to the birth of the new baby. Most of the relatives on both sides were pleased about the union and the pregnancy. The therapist did not dare to ask them to explain the obvious transformation in their relationship. We, too, like Paglia, believe that it is important to remain respectful towards the mystery of male–female bonding.

CHAPTER THREE

Irreverence in institutions: survival

"You're a danger. That's why we kill you. I have nothing against you, you understand, as a man."

Graham Greene, *The Power and the Glory*

P sychiatric hospitals, which try very hard to be helpful in many ways, sometimes inadvertently become only instruments of social control, often in spite of the efforts of therapists working there. By introducing irreverence in the psychiatric hospital, the therapist can help maintain a certain level of flexibility within a context that does, at times, require social control. In an institutional setting the therapist is called upon to obey many contradictory messages—from the clients or the administration, or from socio-political, cultural, or legal factions, and so forth. He cannot obey everyone, for to do so would mean running the risk of losing his efficiency and, perhaps, his "sanity".

The position of the irreverent therapist varies from that of a revolutionary, since the therapist's is not a quest to overcome oppression. The system that the therapist confronts is double-

31

binding, not oppressing. The majority of psychiatric hospitals—as also the majority of other institutions, such as the church, welfare, schools, and so forth—usually support stability and promote dominant cultural values. Thus, accusations are useless. One does not normally ask the institution to change—rather, one attempts to survive within the system. Not by obeying, but by using his own creativity and flexibility to construct a workable meaning system, the therapist can utilize this position of irreverence to help institutions become more flexible and less oppressive, even, perhaps, to dissolve completely. As an analogy, one could say that irreverence on the part of the people and leaders of the former Soviet Union made a superpower dissolve.

The longer a person survives as a therapist, the more he helps his clients to find solutions for themselves. His irreverence as a therapist can be transmitted to the client. The irreverent therapist doubts that any theory or model has or will capture the "true" essence of human behaviour, always reserving the flexibility to challenge the limitations inherent in descriptions imposed by the institution, the client, and, most importantly, by his own biases.

You have to realize that there are some cases where you will not be able to help your client in an institution because to do so may threaten the stability of the institution. There are other instances where patients have chosen—or have been elected into by the family or community of which they are part—a career of mental patienthood. These "professional" patients refuse to change, or they may be in a position that makes it impossible for them to change, and they are unable to leave the institution. Sometimes as a therapist you are caught in conflicting loyalties between the institution and the client, and your solution then is to give up in order to survive. Of course you can choose to risk your survival, for example to lose your job, which may at times be the only ethical alternative. However, most of the time the therapist must survive if he is going to be helpful to anyone.

All of us can remember a case where we know we could have done more, but we did not because we could not find the correct level of irreverence that would allow us to take action and survive. In an aeroplane, for example, when in an emergency the oxygen masks come down, you are told to put the mask on yourself first and then to take care of your child—which is to say, you must survive first, before you can help your child. In institutions therapists must deal with hard-edged situations. The belief that we can help everyone is romantic and naive.

As therapists, however, we do not like to be put in a position of impotence. We are always looking for the opportunities to be loyal both to the institution and to the client. This is where the position of irreverence can be very helpful. Irreverence becomes a healthy alternative. This is what children have to do when a mother wants them to do one thing while the father wants them to do something else. If the child is able to be slightly irreverent to both parents, then he is able to keep his job as a child and be free.

How do you remain flexible in institutions? One way is to maintain an open dialogue with colleagues and clients aimed at understanding and respecting the viewpoint of each. Of course, it is important to remember that the dangers are always the same: the danger of excessive obedience to one side over the other; or, to become wildly irreverent and end up looking insane to both the patient and the institution. This situation reminds us of the teacher in the film, *Dead Poets' Society*, who, in his effort to expand the experience of his students, ended up being scapegoated by his administrative superiors and his students alike.

On the one hand, if you become totally obedient to the institution, you risk appearing like a bureaucratic robot. If, on the other hand, you become totally dedicated and obedient to the client, you may appear to be a revolutionary in the eyes of the institution. In the following case the therapist had to walk a fine line between helping the client while simultaneously not offending the institution. He decided to take the risk of making an intervention that might be deemed appropriate in an out-patient family therapy setting, but difficult to accept in an institutional setting.

The faeces-eating boy

A 14-year-old boy with an IQ of 60 was incarcerated in a state school for numerous delinquent acts, including stealing, drug sale and use, and homosexual prostitution. After a difficult adjustment to institutionalization, the boy began smearing his own faeces all over his body and in his hair, and rolling the faeces up into little balls and eating it. At different times, the staff conceptualized and attempted to work with the boy, first from a psychodynamic, later a behavioural modification, and finally a family-of-origin orientation with no success. The staff could not decide if his behaviour was related more to his retardation or to a psychotic process. Not knowing what to do with him, they were planning to "warehouse" him in a state psychiatric hospital nearby. The therapist, a student of one of the authors, had become very attached to the boy and could not bear to give up on him. She persuaded the administrators to consult with the author. The administrator accepted, in a final attempt to convince the therapist that nothing could be done to help the boy.

The consultant posed a very simple question to the therapist, borrowed from the Brief Therapists at the Mental Research Institution: "In what context would it make perfect sense for this boy to begin eating/smearing his own faeces?" Further inquiry to the therapist revealed that the boy, who was small in stature, was being raped orally and anally by other boys in the correctional school. After he began eating faeces and smearing it on himself, the other boys became repulsed and began avoiding him, calling him crazy. The faeces eating seemed to protect him from being raped.

The question now was, how do you intervene in the situation to help the boy, protect him from assault, and not embarrass the staff of the institution by suggesting that the other therapeutic models were failures? The intervention was twofold. First, the therapist was told to compliment the boy for finding a brilliant way to protect himself when the institution had been unable to do so. He was asked to keep smearing faeces on himself, but to stop eating it because he might get worms. Within a week the boy had stopped eating his faeces, was clean, and was well groomed. The therapist worried that the boy was moving too fast and feared he would be molested again. The boy, however, said the other kids now left him alone because they all still think he is crazy. His crazy reputation in place, the boy could now survive in the institution.

What was irreverent in this instance? One point is timing. The administration was completely frustrated with the situation. Too much staff time was being spent on the treatment of this one child. They were able to be irreverent to their own ability to handle the situation following standard procedures. They were willing, at this point, to listen to a student therapist who offered a suggestion proposed by her teacher, who practised from a model not practised in the institution. The timing was right for an irreverent intervention that would never be allowed at another moment. The consultant, exercising irreverence, was also aware that he might never be invited back to this traditional setting to consult again, even though the intervention was successful. Irreverence was an excellent pain killer for the disappointment of losing a potential consulting job.

How to become a famous "but not rich" psychiatric patient without even trying

Here we describe an unusual situation observed in a psychiatric hospital in Scandinavia where, as we heard the story, a man was hospitalized after threatening to blow up his house while his wife and children were in it. He was then involuntarily committed to a state psychiatric hospital.

A powerful and well-respected psychiatrist, known for his research on the paranoid syndrome, took charge of the treatment. His assessment of the patient was that he represented an unusual and rarefied example of lucid paranoia. The psychiatrist designed a treatment plan based on this assessment and diagnosis, and subsequently wrote several papers related to the progress of the patient.

Disagreeing completely with the diagnosis, the hospitalized man began a long, entrenched battle with the psychiatrist, the hospital, and other professionals at the hospital to force them to change their label. To the psychiatrist and hospital, the harder the man fought against the diagnosis, the more certain they became of its validity. Utterly refusing to accept the diagnosis, the patient naturally refused to accept any kind of medication or in-patient psychotherapy.

After several months of deadlocked attempts to engage him in treatment the psychiatrist prescribed discharge and an out-patient aftercare program. Continuing to refuse to accept the diagnosis, the patient refused to leave until it was changed. He also initiated a law suit against the psychiatrist and the hospital. Thus, a symmetrical escalation began in which the man and the institution were caught in a hopeless stalemate. Neither party could alter its position. It seems to us that the psychiatrist and hospital could not admit a mistake without becoming liable for personal damages as a result of confining him involuntarily. The patient could not accept the diagnosis because to do so would be to deny his legitimate fury against his family. He pitched a tent in the grounds in front of the institution, refusing to leave until his diagnosis was changed.

The case continued to gain notoriety, to the point that when winter came the hospital was compelled for humanitarian rea-sons to invite the patient back inside the hospital. So the patient took on a permanent place of residence in the lobby of the insti-tution, where, to our knowledge, he continues to live in protest.

Even though the hospital still allows the man to reside there and the man continues to refuse to agree with the diagnosis, to us it appears that this battle has faded away. In our opinion the hospital became irreverent to its own position by discontinuing its insistence that he leave, thus allowing him to become almost like a part of the hospital staff and to maintain residence there. The man became irreverent by changing his perception of the institution as a persecutor, accepting it as a nice place to live. Like Bateson's porpoises, both the institution and the patient were able to make a creative leap out of their dilemma.

The catatonic girl

One of the authors was asked to consult on a case involving a catatonic 19-year-old girl in a mental hospital. She had been in this emergency psychiatric hospital for eight months; usually they keep patients for two to four weeks, then send them either for long-term hospitalization or for out-patient care. In this case, the hospital staff could not rid get of her because every time she was ready to leave she created a crisis, becoming catatonic, would not eat, and had to be fed through a tube.

The parents would come every day, pleading for a solution to their daughter's problems. The case had become famous in the community. The psychiatrist in charge of the case was a student of one of the authors and invited him to do a consultation interview. The father, mother, sister, and brother were invited to come to the session. The interview was conducted in a room with a one-way mirror, with the hospital personnel observing.

Sonya, the patient, arrived in a wheel chair pushed by a nurse. The nurse, who was constantly attending the girl, was invited to participate in the session. The girl kept her eyes closed but cried continuously. The mother looked sad and also kept her eyes closed. The father appeared desperate for help for his daughter. The older brother and younger sister looked scared and helpless.

The consultant was perplexed about what to do. The weight of the burden of the girl's problem was now transferred to the therapist, who began to feel overwhelmed and desperate. It seemed as though everyone in the room and behind the mirror was waiting for a magic bullet to dissolve the girl's symptoms. At this point the consultant decided to become irreverent to these impossible demands for a miracle and began to ask, in a mechanical manner, Milan-style questions to the mother, father, sister, brother, and Sonya even though she refused to answer. The questions were the classic ones: How was the relationship between parents and children?; How did Sonya decide to become catatonic?; Who was most upset?; and so on.

Slowly a story emerged. Sonya had run away from home a few times when she was younger. At age 16 she disappeared for several weeks to follow a religious cult, and then she came back. When she returned she was different, and was totally secretive about her experiences. The parents felt she had been raped, or that something similarly terrible had happened to her. Shortly after this the mother and father began to interrogate her about her experiences during her disappearance. The more they interrogated her the more withdrawn and silent she became, eventually becoming completely catatonic. The father was very fond of her, interpreting her silence and withdrawal as a personal rejection, from which he still felt great pain.

During this crisis in the family, the older brother was preparing to get married. The mother was totally preoccupied with planning the wedding. She made it clear that her son's marriage would represent a major loss for her.

The consultant came out of the interview to talk with the team. The dilemma for the consultant was how to formulate a way of using this information in this particular context, in hospital with a dying girl. The team behind the mirror was made up of psychiatrists and psychiatric nurses who were having great doubts that this kind of talk therapy was of any value. He decided to go against the heavy layer of medical pessimism about the patient's prognosis, electing to make a classical Milan intervention, even though he felt it was totally incongruent with the context.

The consultant returned to the session, inviting the attending psychiatrist to accompany him. Looking at the psychiatrist and nurse, he said, "You have been treating this girl wrong. This girl has been here in the hospital because she cannot deal with all the problems at home. The mother is extremely preoccupied in dealing with the impending loss of her son through marriage. Sonya wants to leave her mother alone to handle this mourning. Her being in the hospital also keeps the mind of her father constantly on her, rather than on his wife's sorrow and pain. It is clear that every time she improves a little bit, and you want to send her out of the hospital, she has to get worse. Can you stop doing that? Can you let *her* decide when she's ready to go?" The psychiatrist and nurse, after a brief pause, agreed, saying, "Okay. We will follow your suggestion." As the consultant was about to say goodbye to the family, the mother asked, "That's all you have to say?" "Yes, that's all I have to say." "Don't you have any other suggestion? Any other hospital she can go to? Any therapy to do? Any shock therapy?" The consultant said, "That's what I think. That's my idea as a consultant." The mother was incredulous—"That's what we came here for? We want action!" The consultant responded, "That's all I have to say."

When the consultant joined the group behind the mirror he found the director, three other psychiatrists, and several nurses all dressed in white coats peering at him very sceptically. The consultant carried on with his unusual intervention, which included maintaining a sense of logic and personal dignity with the staff. In an attempt to engage the somewhat detached experts who had been behind the mirror by appealing to their emotions, the consultant made the following comments: "Did you notice that when they were talking about the mother taking care of the brother, the girl woke up a little bit? Also, during the session when I said, `The father is always thinking about her so he leaves the mother alone', the girl was shaking her head a lot? And then, when I said good-bye and tried to give her my hand, she responded a little by opening her eyes and looking at me for the first time?" The staff appeared to be totally unimpressed by what they saw as the consultant's primitive attempt at communicating with a very sick girl by using magical and almost incomprehensible words.

For three weeks the consultant received no news about the patient and was reluctant to ask, not knowing what the hospital staff thought about the interview. Then the psychiatrist called and described what had happened, saying: "Something very interesting has been going on. For three or four days, nothing occurred. Then, the nurses began to notice small changes. Someone on the ward was getting up in the middle of the night, going to the bathroom, then going to bed again. They suspect it was Sonya but said nothing. After four days one morning she got dressed by herself." The nurses were following the prescription given by the consultant that if Sonya began to improve they should ignore her completely. They did not say, "Oh nice of you today. Good that you're up!" They ignored her completely, becoming irreverent to standard procedures.

The patient had improved, but now the attending psychiatrist had another problem. What should be done about getting her discharged, since the consultant's prescription prohibits the following of normal procedures? A decision was made to hold another interview with the family and the staff. In the interview the consultant asked Sonya, who was alert, properly dressed, and smiling, "Now that you have decided to be better what can we do with these people here? They don't know what to do because I told them to ignore you and let you make your own decisions. What should I tell them to do now?" She answered, "I think I'll be ready to leave in two weeks. I want to go for the summer vacation with my family." The consultant responded saying, "Great, that's O.K. with me, but I think we should work together to plan your summer vacation because I am not sure that your parents are up to the intimacy with you that unavoidably will occur during family vacations."

After twenty minutes of negotiations the consultant and the family came up with a plan. On Monday, Sonya will spend the day with her sister. On Tuesday, the day with both her parents. On Wednesday she would spend the day alone. Sonya could visit her brother and his fiancée on Sunday. From Thursday to Saturday the family should act spontaneously. The little sister would be responsible for keeping notes and making sure everyone follows the rules.

Several months later the family came for a follow-up session. Sonya was much improved and the brother had married. Father and mother kept insisting that the family should continue the session, which we agreed to do for six interviews to be held every two months. After the third session Sonya had a relapse and admitted herself to the same hospital. But she was able to recover and be discharged after only two weeks. She was able to recover and continued her successful differentiation.

In terms of irreverence, we have to realize that at certain times in institutions a consultant is given total carte blanche openings to do something unique. At that moment the hospital needed the consultant's help. So they were able to be irreverent to their own expertise and traditions by asking for a systemic consultation. They were aware that their models were not useful to the patient, and they needed the consultant because they did not know what to do with her. They were desperate so they turned to an expert therapist who they thought had some different ideas about how to approach the situation.

The hospital director, being able to be irreverent to his own inability to be helpful, allowed for the consultation. The consultant's ability to be irreverent to what appeared to be an impossible case allowed him to survive the interview.

To enter into such a powerful traditional context and attempt to change an "impossible" case, the consultant had to be irreverent to the superficial modesty that many therapists take pride in, irreverent regarding the hospital staff's refusal to acknowledge the client's ability to be decisive about her life and ability to decide when she can leave. In response to the staff position Sonya was very irreverent to their traditional efforts to help and to hospital discharge procedures.

In order to analyse a situation fully and contextually, one must look at the larger context in which the problem under examination is embedded. For example, in the case under discussion the plan for the hospital to hire the consultant for a future training course was a powerful context marker and complicated the interview for the consultant considerably. The following are some of the questions that were part of the consultant's thinking:

1. Am I being tested before they hire me?
2. Did they give me the worst case in the hospital so I would fail and they would not have to hire me?
3. Am I, without knowing it, an instrument being used by a faction loyal to the Milan School of Systemic Therapy within the hospital to attack the more traditional psychiatric practice?

If you take seriously the first question you become anxious for fear of failing the test. If you fall into the second trap you become depressed over feeling rejected. If you take seriously the third question you end up feeling paranoid. As these questions were passing through the consultant's mind irreverence came to the rescue.

Each institution is a different context, with different rules of survival. Is the institution one that can afford to have its clients get better? In private hospitals where the survival of the institution is dictated by the bottom line, the question of what is in the best interest of the institution must be taken into consideration. In certain institutions there almost seems to be an injunction against even being aware of what you are doing, it is as though there is *one right way* to handle every problem.

Even in public institutions, there is a concern because there is a need for patients to "stay open" (i.e. to remain available for further treatment). If somebody improves too quickly the economic viability in private institutions is threatened. In public institutions the patients are needed to maintain governmental and political support. It is very important for therapists to acknowledge these facts and to keep them in mind when working in such contexts, rather than falling into the trap of complaining about them. This too is an irreverent survival tactic.

We propose that one way to survive, to avoid becoming crazy in the institution, is to become slightly irreverent. We strongly believe that irreverence is a survival tactic that can work in both institutional and out-patient settings. The longer the therapist survives in an institution, the more he becomes a model to inspire the patient to survive without becoming a robot. Our position is that we can only change ourselves; we are unlikely to change the institution. But we can, within the confines of the institution, demonstrate irreverence to the limitations inherent in traditional diagnostic labels by helping the patient to experience "expert descriptions" as but one of many alternative views (i.e. to re-describe the described). We do not propose this as a revolution, rather as a way to survive the many conflicting messages inherent in such contexts.

The overgrown boy

A 16-year-old boy and his family were seen during the boy's stay in a psychiatric hospital. The boy had been hospitalized on and off many times since the age of 12. He had been adopted at birth. His mother had dedicated her entire life to him, whereas the father had always had a cool and critical relationship with him. When the boy reached puberty he began challenging and fighting with his mother constantly.

Between the ages of 11 and 12 he almost doubled in size, which startled the mother. She became so worried about what she experienced as abnormal physical and attitudinal changes that she began taking him to psychiatrists, most of whom spent time coaching her on behavioural modification strategies and biochemical treatment of the son. The more the mother attempted to set limits with the boy, the more his behaviour escalated.

At one point during the boy's long treatment she discovered him in his younger brother's room on top of his brother fully clothed pretending to have sex with him. A week later, while the father was away on a business trip, the mother awoke to discover her son lying in bed with her, clothed in pyjamas, with his arm around her waist. She became frightened, convinced he was making a sexual advance towards her. She got out of bed, coaxed him outside the house, then locked him out. The boy went to the garage and got his father's axe, returned to the door, and attempted to break it down. Hearing the turmoil, a neighbour came over and calmed the boy down.

When the father returned home the boy was hospitalized for the first of many times. Over the next four years the adolescent went through three hospitals. In the first he was both physically and sexually abused by older adolescent patients. In the second hospital he was taken out of the State by irresponsible staff members and set up with a female prostitute. In the third hospital, the patient was depressed and lonely and felt hopeless.

After three years of work with this patient and what turned out to be a very supportive family, we summarized the case in the following way: to the therapist it appeared that the mother was over-involved with the son, always trying to control him, setting limits, and then becoming very frustrated. The father seemed absent much of the time. Talking to the mother, the therapist hypothesized that she was tired of always having to take care of the son. He believed that the mother wanted to take a vacation from trying to control her son, but felt helpless to do so unless "an authority" told her it was alright. The therapist proposed to utilize her idea that he had this authority. Assuming responsibility, he told her to take a temporary vacation from trying to control her son. One consequence was a change in the family pattern. The father became more involved with the son as he never could before.

One might view this instruction as a structural intervention; however, the therapist had no such intent. No preconceived map of how the family should look came into play. The idea for a vacation came from the mother. Using her idea that she needed permission, the therapist gave it.

Three years after entering therapy in the third hospital, the boy was able to return to his home, is getting along well with both his mother and father, and plans to enter studies at a university in the autumn. He has a steady girl-friend and seems to have survived all the "help" he got from professionals at the first two hospitals.

In this instance the therapist responded to the parents' request that he, as an expert, provide guidance for them. Here, the therapist was irreverent to the ideas set forth by Goolishian and other narrative-oriented therapists that the therapist should never take an authoritative or directive position.

Incest between a mother and son

This case involved a 16-year-old boy who was in an institution. The boy was brought to the attention of the juvenile court after he had frequently run away and committed petty crimes in his community. After he was admitted to an institution the following story came out during a family therapy session. He reported that before he began running away his mother had discovered him in his parents' bed having sex with a 14-year-old neighbour. When the mother discovered this she restricted him to the house and started beating him frequently, usually with one of her shoes. Then, after many individual and family sessions, the story finally came out that the boy was having sex with his mother, usually while the father was on the other side of the bed in an alcoholic stupor.

For many months traditional therapy was attempted, with the goals of trying to change the family system, create boundaries, and restructure the family. In individual therapy the incest was frequently discussed in an attempt to help the boy work through what was considered an extremely traumatic event in his life.

Over time, it looked as though this approach was not working. The family continued to appear enmeshed and without boundaries. The more the therapist talked to the boy about incest, the more depressed the boy became. Seven months into treatment, the mother appeared at a family therapy session and reported that this incest event never occurred. Several weeks prior to the session she had gone through a religious conversion experience in a Pentecostal church. She was certain now that the incest experience had been a bad dream—a message to her that she needed Jesus in her life. The father, who had stopped drinking, reported that he now kept a loaded .38 calibre pistol next to their bed. He added that if the son came home again and ever attempted to get into bed with his wife he would kill him. At that point, the boy was not allowed to visit home.

By the mother reporting that the incest was a dream, it confused the boy even more, because for him it was hard reality. He was still stuck. At that moment, the therapist decided that his approach was not working and tried to become irreverent to the traditional approach. The therapist met with a training group he was leading for a consultation. He was very frustrated with the lack of progress in treatment and was worried about the boy's future. A novel reframe emerged from the team consultation.

In the next individual session the therapist introduced the reframe, asking the boy to compare the sexual experience he had with the 14-year-old neighbour and the one he had with his mother. The boy said he felt more relaxed and found the young girl much more physically and romantically appealing than his mother. In talking about the sexual encounters with his mother, he said he was totally confused and "numb".

The therapist told him, very seriously, that the greatest, most brilliant therapist ever, Sigmund Freud, the inventor of the practice of psychoanalysis, said that the fantasy of all men was to sleep with their mother. Most men go through life, on some level, even unconsciously, never being fulfilled because they think their mother would have been the greatest sexual partner. The therapist continued, "It's fantastic that you discovered at a very young age that this is a total myth. Now you can have a very exciting sexual life knowing that your mother was not the best sexual partner for you. Most men never discover this, and for those that do, it usually takes much longer than it has for you."

After this new story was introduced the boy immediately looked relieved. Treatment could move forward to the point that the boy was able to leave the hospital and return to live with his family. Was this some magical kind of metamorphosis?

The therapist had become irreverent against the traditional form of therapy that insisted children involved in incest required years of therapy to work through the trauma of such a devastating event. The traditional therapy was pushing the boy further into depression, helping him feel like a deviant, a criminal, a pervert. The therapist was willing to take the risk of questioning the prevalent (and "politically correct") approach to the treatment of incest by introducing this reframe, rather than sticking with an approach that he realized was hurting the boy. This redescribing of the situation helped the boy work his way out of the institution and get on with his life.

Three years later the boy came back to the therapist for a friendly visit. When questioned about his family he said that he had left his family, had experienced many good sexual relationships with other women, had joined the army, and was engaged to be married.

In this case the irreverence does not lie only in the reframing of the situation. It also involves being able to come out of the traditional model while working with very serious circumstances. The institution was able to accept this kind of intervention because at that point the staff was totally frustrated with the lack of progress, and the goal of the institution was to help the boy return to the community and lead a successful life.

We need frequent consultation and dialogue with colleagues to protect clients from the consequences of our own rigidity, and to help us avoid becoming locked into one right story. Irreverence is a flexible state of mind, which includes being irreverent to reverence for one's own convictions.

To be irreverent is not easy. Sometimes the therapist has to be patient, waiting until the time is right. The institution involved must be at a point where, through frustration at their own lack of progress, the staff can tolerate more dramatic interventions, as in the case of Sonya and of the boy who was having sex with his mother. In many instances there is a time of grace during which change can happen in institutions, if the therapist can exploit it. In both instances, if the therapist had used the irreverent approach at the very beginning, he would have run the risk of being discredited by the institution.

To reiterate, working in institutions is a lot like working with families. You have to allow the system to push its own premise to the point of absurdity. Organizations, regardless of size, are the same in this respect. Families or larger organizations are all systems. There is a tendency towards rigidity or stasis and towards self-correction. At the same time, it is equally important to remember that when therapists are committed so strongly to their own premises that they cannot consider other ways of looking at the situation, they get into trouble, blind to the moment of grace and the opportunity for change. Following Prigogine and Stengers (1984), we can speculate that all systems go through periods of instability during which time change is possible. Unfortunately, many of us have been trained only to recognize and describe stability. So we frequently miss the opportunities available to evoke change during chaotic states. We believe that irreverence is a position that allows us to open our eyes to these opportunities.

CHAPTER FOUR

Suggestions for training

"It's so easy to kill real people in the name of some
damned ideology or other, once the killer can abstract
them in his own mind into being symbols, then he needn't
feel guilty for killing them since they're no longer human
beings."

James Jones,
in a *Paris Review* interview with Nelson W. Aldrich, Jr.

Although we each train and supervise separately and in
different contexts, we have found that the training
problems we deal with are very similar. Furthermore,
our personal philosophies of supervision correspond. Despite
these similarities, fortunately no two of our training programs
are exactly identical. Gianfranco is Co-Director of a four-year
training program in systemic therapy with about 100 students, in
Milan, Italy. Gerry directs a small, private, two-year training program in systemic therapy in Atlanta, Georgia. Wendel teaches

and supervises systemic therapy in a two-year training program with about thirty students, in Monroe, Louisiana.

Generally speaking the training models we have followed reflected a fairly traditional approach, heavily influenced by Gregory Bateson, Don D. Jackson, the Brief Therapy Project at the Mental Research Institute, and, later, the influences of second-order cybernetic and narrative epistemologists.

Trainees are first required to review the relevant theoretical and clinical literature, spending an extended period of time reading about first- and second-order cybernetics, systemic therapies, narrative approaches, and so forth. Only after this lengthy period spent on intellectual work and getting familiar with the ideas do they begin their supervised live work with families. At this point, we then begin to look closely at the trainees' epistemological premises.

This is the traditional orientation to training students in a model. This training strategy comes from a belief that being an effective therapist requires a basic literacy in the existing knowledge of cybernetic theory and clinical practice. We continue to be convinced of the utility of a thorough knowledge of specific models or orientations to practise before venturing into the more complex and lively experience of clinical practice. This is where you can begin to utilize the position of irreverence.

More recently, however, we have begun to expand our thinking about the traditional training approach, finding that it is often effective to start the other way around. At a number of workshops where we have presented these ideas students voiced a desire to begin immediately to practise therapy from a position of irreverence before getting too bogged down in the tyranny of different theoretical dogmas.

Isomorphic to the practice of therapy, training can begin with asking students about their ideas about clients. Once students begin to reflect upon their ideas about the case, and discuss with other students their biases (which we prefer to call prejudices), a confluence of different ideas begins to emerge. They begin to become curious about other stories. We agree with Keeney and Ross's position (1985) that the job of the trainer is one of gate-keeping. To us gate-keeping is leading the group members to

articulate many different ideas and biases about the case, affirm-
ing each perspective, but then synthesizing the various hypotheses and ideas in such a way as to be coherent with the specifics
of the case while at the same time offering different alternatives.
An important part of this process is to avoid getting bogged
down in the content of the plots offered by different trainees,
emphasizing instead the ability of each student to observe patterns in the client's story. Like a master chef, the trainer's task is
to continue to stir the soup, breaking up symmetrical exchanges
when they appear. It is our experience that symmetrical exchanges occur when emphasis is given more to content than to
process. The trainer mixes together the ingredients of the conversation, not dictating the direction but contributing to the emerging story. Of course, the trainer must at times honour his contract
with the trainees by exerting his position as instructor and being
the one who makes the final synthesis. But, ideally, we attempt
to create an egalitarian process.

A successful training group ordinarily starts out with the
trainer taking more of a traditional student–teacher role, being
more directive about which aspects of the emerging story will
prevail. As the group evolves the trainer is able to move to the
more collaborative role of gate-keeper.

One great value of this approach to training is that by ferreting
out the student's ideas initially, we can understand their personal prejudices immediately and they begin to understand their
own prejudices as well.

Like that of the philosopher Gadamer (1987), it is our belief
that the notion of prejudices is not in and of itself a negative
thing, and it is useful for therapists to understand where their
prejudices are. According to Gadamer:

> It is not so much our judgements as it is our prejudices that con-
> stitute our being. This is a provocative formulation, for I am
> using it to restore to its rightful place a positive concept of preju-
> dice that was driven out of our linguistic usage by the French and
> the English Enlightenment. It can be shown that the concept of
> prejudice did not originally have the meaning we have attached
> to it. Prejudices are not necessarily unjustified and erroneous, so

that they inevitably distort the truth. In fact, the historicity of our existence entails that prejudices, in the literal sense of the word, constitute the initial directedness of our whole ability to experience. Prejudices are biases of our openness to the world. They are simply conditions whereby we experience something—whereby what we encounter says something to us. This formulation certainly does not mean that we are enclosed within a wall of prejudices and only let through the narrow portals those things that we can produce a pass saying, "Nothing new will be said here." Instead we welcome just that guest who promises something new to our curiosity. But how do we know the guest whom we admit is one who has something new to say to us? Is not our expectation and our readiness to hear the new also necessarily determined by the old that has already taken possession of us?

Before therapists are ever introduced to theoretical and clinical models to be prejudiced by, it is helpful for them to understand that they are already organized by the general prejudices they hold. As Weakland says, the tendency for people to see what they already believe is pervasive. Family therapy is very different from other sciences for the simple reason that we are all, in some way, experts about families. That is where we all grow up. Family therapy is unlike sciences, such as the study of the physiology of the human body, the study of astronomy, or other disciplines that require mastery of a larger body of knowledge not familiar to most of us. In our profession, we hypothesize that personal premises influence the model of therapy that people choose. Prejudices are like heat-seeking missiles that home in on models that confirm pre-existing views of the world.

It is amazing that in the therapy market-place any prejudice can be developed into a theoretical model to be packaged and sold to prospective followers. If you love thinking about family history and are fascinated by diagrams you gravitate towards Bowen. If you are fascinated by intricate plots, conspiracies, and betrayal, you discover Selvini. If you are loyal to your grandparents' parents, you find Boszormenyi-Nagy. If you are still nostalgic about father being in charge, Minuchin or Haley are easily available. If you believe that loss is fundamental, Norman Paul is the guy for you. If you believe it is all a matter of family development you fall in love with Carter and McGoldrick. If you believe oppressive patriarchies are the source of all evil, then Goldner or Michael White are ready to offer a well-articulated theory. If you are still a child of the 1960s and believe love conquers all, Virginia Satir is your cup of tea. All of these people, and all other inventors of therapy models, were brilliant masters at creating elegant and useful approaches based upon some prejudice offered by the culture.

These models have all been useful in helping many people, students and clients alike. As clinicians and trainers, these prejudices and theories are all we have to work with. The post-modern position is to be able to employ a prejudice that is useful, to discard prejudices when they are not useful, and to be able to juxtapose other prejudices in forming hybrids.

How to traumatize a beginning therapist

Training is a very good context for supervisors and students alike to become aware of and question their own prejudices. An example comes to mind of the potentially profound consequences of the supervisors' and students' fundamental premises. A young female student in a marriage and family therapy programme started working with clients at a centre that provided services to battered women. A number of her first clients entered therapy with incest as the presenting problem. The student became very anxious, was easily upset, and became very unsure of herself in therapy. The supervisor responded in what is becoming an all too-frequent manner. As the student became increasingly anxious, not knowing what to do in therapy with the emotionally laden problem of incest, she experienced an empathic reaction to the pain she saw in the clients. She became convinced that she must have been a victim of incest herself when she was young, even though she had no recollection of any event remotely resembling an incestuous relationship at any time during her life.

The intern began talking to anyone who would listen to her. A number of her fellow students, several female faculty at the school, professors, and a supervisor who adhered to one of the prevalent psychodynamic models about incest, reinforced the intern's self-interpretation that the only explanation for her emotional upset when working with this population must be that she was molested when she was young, and the traumatic experience was so terrible that she had blocked it out of her memory. With very little supporting facts to substantiate such a theory, and at the direction of her supervisor, the intern entered into therapy with a therapist to help her uncover the alleged early-life trauma so that it could be worked through.

After months of therapy focusing on helping her remember the incest that "must" have occurred, she continued to have no memory of such a trauma ever having happened. However, because an early trauma of molestation was the only explanation seriously considered by the supervisor, therapist, and others in whom the intern confided, she was continuously told that the only way she would ever deal with the situation was through intensive therapy focusing on helping her remember the trauma so that it could be worked though. She must have been traumatized when young. This was the only plausible way she could explain to herself why she became so upset working with this population.

An alternative explanation did exist to which no one gave serious consideration. The intern's emotional reaction is easily understood if the system theory premise that all behaviour makes sense when thought about in context is applied. The trainee was a young, sensitive woman who had no experience of working with very emotional situations. Feeling intense compassion for the clients and very unsure of herself, she read all the literature on incest she could find to try to understand the situation. All of these actions reinforced the popular theory that if something is upsetting for someone, it may be a personal issue for him.

She was under the supervision of a supervisor who was convinced of this dictum: if a clinician has difficulty with an issue, it is evidence that it must be a personal issue. The beginning therapist was reinforced at every turn with the idea that she must have been molested in such a traumatic way that she could not remember it. According to this theory, the less a person can remember, the more traumatic the molestation must have been.

The student, afraid of not knowing how to help her clients, constantly worried that she might be doing more harm than good. Under the tutorage of an individual therapist, who specializes in working with survivors of incest, this intern spent months unsuccessfully trying to remember a trauma that in all likelihood never occurred. Finally, after much money spent on months of therapy, the father, who was paying for the therapy, refused to fund any more treatment. In light of the trainee's absolute failure in remembering a traumatic early-life molestation, the therapist began to entertain with the intern the possibility that she may never have been molested at all. Perhaps she was a sensitive human being reacting intensely to the pain she saw in the clients she was working with. One idea we have is that the father's decision to stop paying helped the therapist change his hypothesis that the intern was a victim of incest. Alternatively, is it possible that the therapist interpreted the father's willingness to pay for the therapy as an admission of guilt? Who knows, this is just speculation.

What comments can we make about this case? According to our biases both the therapist and the student believed in the reality of their own prejudices so ardently that they became stuck. Both therapist and student were caught in an inquisition to discover the truth, instead of seeing the intern's anxious behaviour as a natural reaction to the problems of her clients, as a pattern of communication between the intern and her clients. If you can recognize the style of relationship materializing between an intern and client as an emergent system, you can then find a way to utilize it therapeutically.

Next, we will look at a training situation in which the intern's prejudices were utilized by the team to create a therapeutic intervention.

The incompetent mother

A student in Milan emerged from a session being conducted with a mother and two unruly children to converse with her colleagues behind the mirror: "I think this lady is totally incompetent to be a mother. She's very naive, she doesn't know what to do to control her children." The team asked, "What do you want to do?" "Well, I feel like helping her, giving her some instructions. She needs something, she doesn't seem to know anything." To this announcement, the therapists and consultants in the group replied: "To give instructions to people does not work. It is not helpful. It doesn't work." The debate behind the screen continued: "I like to give instructions/Instructions are useless." The resolution was, "Okay, use this kind of difference and talk to the patient about it." The student re-entered the therapeutic session and stated, "Look, you were very successful in convincing me that you are incompetent. I believe you, and I feel as if I should give you some instructions. My colleagues behind the mirror say to give instructions is useless, it is against their theory. They have a systemic theory that doesn't permit them to think that way. So I made a deal with my colleagues. They give me permission to believe that you are incompetent, but only for the next three months, and I must take the consequences of my belief. In three months we will discuss it again." The therapist then gave her some simple instructions. Three months later the patient, who had been following instructions, appeared to be improving in her behaviour. The student said: "My colleagues are curious to know why you obeyed my instructions. In systemic theory, people don't obey. Why did you obey?" To this the patient replied: "I obeyed because I like you better than I like the people behind the mirror." The patient changed the level of the conversation.

In this example the student therapist was irreverent towards the idea that you cannot give instructions, even in therapy. By saying, "My colleagues believe in systemic therapy . . .", she introduced an element of playfulness. It is irreverent to say, "I choose to believe that you are incompetent. You gave me this message and I choose to believe, which is irreverent to the truth. There is no truth in this situation. The question of incompetence or competence is secondary, it is part of a relationship. You convinced me and I choose to believe; therefore, I'm irreverent towards my colleagues, who believe in systemic therapy." It is also expressing irreverence towards the patient to say, "I believe you're incompetent, but in reality, it's just a message that you give me".

Working with a team can be an efficient way to utilize the resonance between what the therapist is experiencing and what seems to be happening within the family. On many occasions, however, therapists may not have the luxury of a readily available team. If a therapist is working alone, then it is important that he is tuned into his own discomfort when the case is not progressing. Usually, the explanation for the lack of progress is that the therapist is stuck in content and unable to see the process. Alternatively, the therapist may have lost his ability to be irreverent to his own prejudice and therefore lacks the capacity for curiosity for different ways of thinking about the situation. Or, the therapist may have become too obedient to the work context in which he is practising.

With time therapists become aware of their idiosyncratic ways of manifesting discomfort. Some therapists develop back pain or headaches. Others become restless. Some have strong fantasies of clients not showing up, or suffer self-doubt about not having made the right choice of profession, and so forth. Whatever symptom appears, the therapist can experience it as a cue to look for help. We are absolutely sure that all therapists know at least one colleague with whom they can discuss the case, or show a videotape or audio recording to, or invite to observe a session. It is our experience that no elaborate description or inordinate amount of time is required to grasp the non-productive pattern in which one is stuck. Usually such patterns are very similar. For example, you want to control too much, so the patient goes out of control. Or, you want to teach too much, so the patient becomes a slow learner, and so on.

The lady who could not stop coming to therapy

After two years of couple therapy, a couple was discharged from therapy. Subsequently the wife called saying she wanted to talk. She came in but had nothing of any apparent relevance to say. The therapist handled it as a follow-up, and the woman left. She returned again in six months, still with no problems but just wanting to talk. Six months later she came again. Later she called yet again, asking for another session. The therapist felt uneasy about the case, so he asked permission from the woman to hold the session in the presence of some colleagues, to which she agreed. The therapist invited some first-year students to be observers and asked them to watch out for anything happening that could explain the chronic therapy pattern.

About ten minutes into the session the students called the therapist and said the situation was very clear to them. From the behaviour of the therapist, the way he treated the couple, the way he shook their hands, the position of sitting, expressions on his face, and so forth, it was quite obvious that the therapist felt sorry for them, especially the wife. This expression of empathy based on pity could be an explanation for why the therapy could not stop. The therapist, upon hearing this description, agreed completely and was shocked that he had been unable to see this pattern before. On most occasions it is not a question of repression, or unresolved issues in your family, or whatever, that makes you unable to see a pattern. What you are able to see depends on the position you hold in the system. Culturally it is quite easy for a therapist to experience himself as being a caring person, without realizing that the caring can become pity, which in turn subtly implies a disrespectful attitude towards the client, which we call, in our jargon, negative connotation. We know that the use of negative connotation can be an excellent glue to keep people stuck to each other.

In fact, in situations where it seemed therapeutically appropriate, we have suggested to parents who do not want to let their children go, to mildly insult and put their children down verbally to ensure that they never leave home. Of course the art of insulting their children has been refined by parents over millions of years. Therapeutic insulting is a finely honed skill—because if too brazen, the clients never come back and you can't pay your bills!

The sad young therapist

A young woman was involved in a clinical internship at a large psychiatric clinic. She was studying at a university that strictly adhered to the psychodynamic model of psychotherapy, and she was expected to enter into psychodynamic clinical training. One of the authors noticed this woman sitting alone in her office one day looking dejected. When questioned about what was going on she replied that she had been training at the clinic under the guidance of a psychodynamically oriented supervisor for the past four months. Earlier in the day she had received one of her first evaluations by her supervisor. The evaluation was to be reported back to her university. In the report the supervisor commented that at this point in her training she had been unable to engage clients in the initial phase of long-term, insight-oriented therapy. Many of her cases were seen for only four to six sessions, during which she and the patient felt the problems had improved. The supervisor viewed this as indicating the intern's lack of ability to engage people in a long-term therapeutic relationship so that insight into their psychopathology and repetitive problematic patterns could be brought forth and worked through.

The intern reported that she was very hurt and confused by this. Based on this feedback from her supervisor she was even contemplating dropping out of the training and university altogether. The author, realizing he might be crossing a supervisory boundary, nevertheless felt it might be useful to this demoralized beginning therapist to share a story that might help her feel better.

He said it looked like she had developed a natural and intuitive ability to work briefly with clients. However, in order to gain professional credentials, she must complete the degree programme at the university, as well as the internship training under the direction of her current supervisor. His recommendation to her was, for the moment, to attempt to learn the psychodynamic model that many people, including patients, view as having great value—a model from which you can take ideas—and a model which, hopefully, she could draw from throughout her career. On the other hand, it was hoped she could maintain her natural and intuitive ability to work briefly with people without creating tremendous dependency on her for ideas and insights. His opinion as a supervisor was that this gift is rare and, in many ways, the clinical practice that could result from it is far more sophisticated than traditional psychodynamic therapy. Yet, at the same time she was encouraged to try to have some kind of belief in her supervisor and the psychodynamic model during the next two years in order to complete her training.

To us, this story represents the use of what we described earlier as *temporary certainty*, where the student, in order to complete (one might say survive) the training program, must temporarily believe in it for the necessary time. At the end of that time she would have the freedom to recoup her natural gifts for brief therapy.

The temporary anorexia of a student

A young student was talking to a couple of middle-aged parents after their two daughters had been asked to leave the session. One of the daughters, aged 17, had been anorectic and had been slightly improving for some time. The general opinion in the supervision group behind the mirror was that the couple was always so involved with the daughters that they had no time to enjoy themselves together.

The therapist was asking routine questions such as what they were going to do when their daughters become independent, or how their leaving would affect their relationship, and so forth. The parents seemed to agree with the opinion of the therapist that their life was somewhat empty without the children. But, just at that moment, the husband revealed that he was planning to invite the wife to the opera the next week and he expected to enjoy it. The therapist immediately snapped: "I don't believe you will, you are so used to being only parents that it is hard to imagine you enjoying yourself without the children." The people behind the mirror began to worry. Soon after, the mother mentioned that the day before she had taken her husband shopping for the first time and they almost enjoyed themselves. Again, the therapist responded saying: "I don't believe you enjoyed yourselves. You have never done that before!"

The therapist was immediately called behind the mirror and asked to describe what she felt about the couple. She said "I think they are making fun of me. They really have nothing between them and are only trying to show me how they can function without the children, but I don't believe them." The therapist talked in a frenzy for about five minutes. When the turn to make comments came to the observing group, one of the members said: "It is very clear to me that our colleague has taken the place of Maria, the anorectic daughter, who for years has been interfering with the life of the parents any time they wanted to do something without her."

The therapist was struck by this observation and left the room without comment. A few minutes later she appeared in the therapy room where she said to the couple: "My colleagues behind the mirror noticed that I behave like your daughter when I say that I don't believe you can enjoy yourselves without her. I would like to ask you to end this session now because I fear that if we stay here I am going to do it again. My wish to do it is stronger than I am and I need some time to overcome the temptation to do it again." Smiling, the husband and wife got up, hugged her, and left saying: "Please give our regards to your friends behind the mirror."

A month later they came back, again alone, and began a lively conversation with our therapist who, this time, was talking in a very comfortable manner with the couple. The conversation touched upon many interesting subjects. We discovered that the life of these two people was much richer than anyone in the therapeutic team had imagined. The question was now: Who had made the change—the couple or the therapist?

CHAPTER FIVE

Some considerations for research

"If a man cannot forget, he will never amount to much."

Kierkegaard, *Either/Or*

O ne does not have to look at research as an attempt to find the truth. Our position is that we will never find the essence of psychopathology, or human suffering, but that the research data is always useful in terms of building hypotheses.

One of the apparent dangers of post-modern thought is the implication that all existing theories are no longer held to be "true", and, therefore, they become useless. Post-modernism suggests that we should question all things. And yet we find great value in traditional research logic in as much as it is like any other perspective, any other belief. The question is not whether it is true, but whether we can make use of it in the practise of therapy.

We could say our reality is a very well organized, self-verifying experience, with which we must deal every day, whether or

63

not it exists separate from ourselves, or is created by us. Still it is the reality we describe, in which we can find patterns, rules, repetitions.

When we conduct research, then, or when we study the existing research findings, we can use these "findings" as hypotheses. One is naturally careful not to carry these "findings" or "truths" to an extreme point of view, where one attempts to fit the family into a claimed research "truth". One has the freedom to look at a research finding as a useful idea, and at the same time be able to discard it if it does not fit a family or client.

Suppose a therapist is working in a traditional setting—for example, a shelter for battered women—and the professionals there have access to all of the statistical research available on battered women. If a person comes from a family in which the father was involved in an incestuous relationship with that person, and his father was involved in an incestuous relationship with him, and they all happen to drink too much and have been labelled alcoholics by an expert, then, on the basis of that research, the therapist "knows" that not only is the client at the shelter a battered person, but also probably an alcoholic and possibly a child abuser. This is an example of an "empirical" paradigm that can become a predominant model for working with incest. By and large, front-line therapists do not see research findings like those described above as generalizations or hypotheses. Rather, far too often such research findings are accepted as "truth" handed down from above—something that is not to be questioned.

For instance, take a therapist who never reads research, who works with the same clients, and who never diagnoses them as having tendencies for alcoholism or child abuse. This therapist could appear incompetent to colleagues more versed in research stories, regardless of how capable he is in working with this population.

From an irreverent perspective, how can we handle the kind of empirical data outlined above? If you begin to believe too strongly in the truth of the research, then you run the risk of creating a self-fulfilling prophecy. It is dangerous to believe too ardently in research constructions, seductive though this may be, especially if your institution values these findings. It can also be dangerous to avoid research out of fear of falling in love with the findings, and thus losing the ability to see humans rather than research probabilities.

The danger is not in the research but in the notion that if a therapist believes too ardently in the research findings, as though it is truth, then he is unable to see anything else. When looking at the client's family, it may come out that the grandfather and mother were alcoholics. The belief of the therapist then is that there is a great chance that the client will become an alcoholic. In therapy with this client, the therapists may automatically perceive him to be an emerging alcoholic. The clinician loses the ability to see the client from any other perspective. The clinician, in this case, tends to see only things about the client that match the research, losing interest in being curious about other aspects of the person. His head is so full of prejudices from the research that he could end up co-constructing psychopathology that does not even exist in the client's experience.

Let us use another example. Margaret Hoopes and James Harper (1987) have written several excellent books on sibling position indicating that research shows that certain patterns of behaviour are evident in children according to whether they are the first-born, second-born, third-born, etc. Reading this book a therapist can find the conclusions fascinating. A danger we see is that people can become one-dimensional caricatures of human beings. The script that assigns roles to the children should come from the family and not from a research book, no matter how frequently a given script shows up in different families. We want to appreciate the research rather than worship at its altar.

There are two prevalent types of research: quantitative and qualitative. There are many quantitative research studies—such as those that have focused on the phenomenon of alcoholism—that have studied the number of children who become alcoholics whose parents were alcoholics, or the number of children abused by parents who become abusing parents, and so forth. When we look at studies such as these, we also have to remember that there is another percentage of people who do not become alcoholics or abusers. Our curiosity is directed towards the exceptions, who cannot *not* exist and are equally important, perhaps even more so.

Then there is descriptive or qualitative research such as research that describes certain relationship patterns prevalent in specific family organizations such as single-parent families. Such data might highlight the forming of a more marriage-like relationship between a parent and child, for example; or, the relationship between acting-out behaviour of children and the sharing of parental responsibility in blended families.

It is important to take into consideration that these two types of research can be useful to the process of building and testing hypotheses.

If a therapist has training in traditional research and then is trained to be slightly irreverent all the time, some very interesting research could result. When as a therapist you see a client, instead of looking at how he or she fits the existing research, you should look for how the client disobeys the rules of research. You can train yourself to look at how clients do not fit the data—at the exceptions. In the case an of alcoholic, you could say to the client, "The research says you are supposed to be an alcoholic. How come you're not?" Or, "How does it feel to have all these experts predicting you are going to become a hopeless alcoholic? Or an abuser?" Or, "How respectful do you think you have to be to this evidence?" Or, "How loyal a citizen are you to the prevailing culture?" Thus, the therapist and the client can becomes curious about what does not fit the research, rather than have their behaviour dictated by statistics that by their very nature relate to conglomerates of populations and could have nothing to do with a specific human being sitting in the therapist's office.

Irreverence often involves sailing against the prevailing wind. Not just to be oppositional, but to have the freedom as therapists to look for things in the family that the research does not emphasize (i.e. adaptive capabilities, resources, etc.). In this way we become very curious about the exceptions to the predominant data informing our work. This is an idea that also underlies the work of such people as John Weakland (1989), Steve De shazer (1982), and Michael White (1989).

At the same time as being irreverent therapists, we must also feel free to take the empirical data seriously. People with integrity devote their lives to the study of family systems and their data should always be considered as a valuable source of hypotheses in the field, not just as some researcher's construction.

Traditional research is useful in making generalizations about large populations, but says very little about individual families. It is, however, an excellent resource for analysing the cultural context in which the family exists.

What we would love to see are studies of the deviations of research data. In other words, we need more research studying families where, for example, the parents are alcoholics and the children do not become alcoholics; or families where parents are totally uneducated, the father is an alcoholic, and the child ends up going to Harvard. This kind of research, we think, would broaden our view of family organizations. Traditional research, by its very nature, tends to flatten complex systems like families by bringing forth what is common and predictable.

Let us suppose for the sake of argument that 80% of children of alcoholics become alcoholic, and very often the one who comes to the office is one of this 80%. Believing this to be true, the therapist now becomes confirmed in his opinion, then transmits this idea to the client, even a sober client. We tend to forget the other 20%, as though they do not exist because there is no research about them. Remembering about the deviations from the research data is not always easy. We must keep in mind, learning from the constructivist position, that we bring forth what we believe.

Much of present-day research places an extraordinary amount of emphasis on statistical studies, such as, "How many people become this way? . . . What are the similarities in background of people who become this way? . . ." etc. We would like to propose research asking questions such as: "How come many children from so-called severely dysfunctional families turn out fine?" Or, "What kind of patterns of relationship exist in the so-called problematic family that can be held responsible for producing children that do well?" This kind of research would give insight into which aspects of the system to work with and amplify. This would be one way to conduct research on phenomena that have been described in systemic theory in terms of "multi-finality and equi-finality". How can people coming from very similar beginnings end up being very different, or come from very different beginnings end up having very similar problems.

We enjoy looking at the exceptions, the nonconformists, the people who drink heavily or have had psychotic episodes and are extremely productive in other aspects of their lives. We believe that some of the most insightful research on exceptions now exists in the field of literary biographies where the exceptions as well as problems are examined and contextualized. For example, the author William Faulkner, who drank heavily into the night and is rumoured to have had several love affairs, and yet remains one of America's premiere novelist. Or, the statesman Winston Churchill, who seemed to go out of his way to break all taboos about eating, drinking, and smoking and yet lived an extraordinarily productive and long life.

One criticism of this kind of research proposal might be that as therapists we should be concerned about "pathology". After all, some would say that we are in the business of helping people overcome "pathology". One response to this concern is the idea that pathology is, in large part, constructed in the relationship between the myths, prejudices, and beliefs held within the larger culture about what is healthy or not healthy, beautiful or ugly, moral or immoral; and the individual's struggle to make sense of and survive within these often contradictory injunctions. Obviously, the therapist is in a unique position to help co-construct "pathology", or to dissolve it. The convictions and prejudices of the therapist and client alike are part and parcel of the construction.

An example

One of the authors designed a research project in Milan to see if just asking circular questions, without the use of other interventions, with a family in a session had an effect on future behaviour. Some students from the Milan School of systemic family therapy contacted three different Public General Hospitals in the area, each with twenty-bed psychiatric units and each attached to active out-patient services, and asked the administrators if a research could be conducted. The administrators agreed and even offered to fund it. Twenty patients with a diagnosis of schizophrenia of at least two year's duration, between the ages of 18 and 25, all heavy users of the hospital's services (pharmacological, in-patient, and out-patient) were chosen at random for participation in the research. They all had been under pharmacological as well as psychological therapy for some years, including individual, group, and family therapy for some.

How the research was to be presented to the staff and to the clients was deemed crucial. The question to be asked was formulated as follows. To the doctor in charge we asked: "Can you let your patient be part of a research project?" We posed the same question to the families. "By asking simple questions, the research is going to inquire, Why has this particular person in this family became a patient?" We emphasized to both the physician and the family that we were conducting research, and *not* doing any therapy. We stressed that we did not want to help anybody. Rather, we just wanted to conduct research and needed their cooperation in answering a few questions.

A group of expressed-emotion researchers (EER, an instrument and method for measuring affect in families and individuals) were asked to examine the families before, in the middle of, and at the end of the research project. The study was to last six months, with one encounter with the family once a month. The EER examiners would also interview a control group consisting of twenty families with similar diagnosis not involved in the study. The two groups—the research students and the EER people—did not have contact or communicate with each other during the entire research project.

We anticipated that the families would be reluctant to participate since no therapy was being offered and there was no obvious pay off for them. At the beginning of the project, it was surprising that although one family refused to participate, the others were very happy to come. Possibly the latter were so tired of being therapized that they found research a relief, or feared sanctions if they did not cooperate with the institution on which they depended heavily. The research therapists also enjoyed their work, possibly because they were not responsible for providing therapy. They did not have to make hypotheses and interventions. After 45 minutes of asking circular questions, the sessions were ended with a simple statement: "See you in a month."

The questions asked during the interviews were the classical Milan circular questions, such as:

1. Who is closer to whom?
2. How did the relationship between mother and father change since the patient decided to become schizophrenic?
3. What changes do you expect if you decide to get better?
4. Who would be more upset?
5. Suppose your sister took your place what would happen?

The therapists were organized in teams of two, one in the therapy room and one behind the one-way mirror. The job of those behind the mirror was to control the wish of the therapist in the room to give interpretations, injunctions, or rituals to the family. This was a very difficult task because the therapist's temptation to *do something* "therapeutic" was sometimes overwhelming.

About half-way through the project a point was reached, during a regular meeting of the research group, where the interviewers complained of extreme frustration at being forbidden from doing something to help. The supervisor was convinced that they had to try to keep faith to the non-interventive nature of the research project. By the time the project ended, however, it was apparent that the rule had probably been broken on a few occasions. In one instance, for example, it was discovered after the fact that one interviewer could not help himself from making the following statement to a family: "If we were not doing research I would give you the following suggestions" (then a few suggestions specific to that family were offered). "But don't do anything about it because we are only doing research, not therapy" (a classic paradoxical statement).

The result of the research was a dramatic reduction of rehospitalization for the schizophrenic members during the research period—62% fewer relapses than the control group. Furthermore, there was a significant lowering of expressed emotion in the research group. There was a 5% drop-out rate at the end of the period, compared to 25% in the control group.

What we learned from this experience was the following. It is hard for a clinician to distinguish between when he is doing therapy and when he is doing research. The clinician is always watching what the effects of his actions are on the client, and comparing them with what he already knows. Therefore, in one sense, his actions or interventions could be called research. The researcher cannot avoid being drawn into co-constructing a new reality as soon as he gets in touch with a human system. Therefore, he becomes a clinician. Was this project therapy smuggled as research? Or was it research smuggled as therapy?

CHAPTER SIX

Random closing meditations

> Why is it possible to learn more in ten minutes about the
> Crab Nebula in Taurus, which is 6,000 light-years away,
> than you presently know about yourself, even though
> you've been stuck with yourself all your life?
>
> Walker Percy, *Lost in the Cosmos.*

A s we reflect back on this journey we have taken together, we find to our surprise how conservative the
idea of irreverence really is. Sailing in these sometimes
remote and choppy waters, we find that on occasion we yearn
for the safe harbours that some of our predecessors represent for
us.

And so, as this irreverent excursion comes to an end, we find
ourselves reflecting upon the many brilliant and creative people
who have influenced our thinking and practice and to whom
we would like to pay tribute. Gregory Bateson, with his brilliant
stories. Who can equal the wisdom that he shared in his life?

Don Jackson, whose spirit and influence pervades not only our own orientation, but the entire field of family therapy which he helped create. Harry Stack Sullivan, the too-often overlooked inventor of interpersonal thinking, the first to recognize that we are all much more human than anything else, and the well from which so many people have drawn sustenance. R.D. Laing, with his total honesty and ability to see the knots into which all humans are capable of getting entangled yet not even be aware of. Freida Fromm-Reichmann, another near-forgotten but profoundly influential figure in the pre-history of family therapy. Milton Erickson, with his utter conviction that we can help people change. Jay Haley, who continues to keep the flame of strategic theory burning in the face of the strong winds of the narrative movement. Harry Goolishian, who has the ability to bring the field of family therapy almost to a standstill with the simple, yet beautiful, reminder that we must not forget to listen to people again before we impose solutions. Mara Selvini Palazzoli, with her incredible belief in the power of therapy as well as her forceful conviction that man is a strategic animal. John Weakland, with his keen perceptive and conceptual abilities, helping us to appreciate the profoundly playful implications of the dictum that "One thing leads to another". Lynn Hoffman, with her ability to synthesize many complex ideas and put them into a comprehensible, if sometimes controversial, form.

As is so often the case with many enjoyable conversations as they wind down, yet another interesting notion comes to mind— that of oscillation, the pendulum-like experience that many of us experience during our careers between total cynicism (for example, of the traditional, biological orientation to psychiatry) and a naive enthusiasm for such beliefs as the almost magical potency of therapeutic strategy. Our position reflects the desire not to be so naive as to think we can change all the problems our clients face, but at the same time not to fall into the cynical trap that we can do nothing when faced with difficult problems. Rather, to have the freedom to take action. To somehow be able to survive the devastation and disappointment that sometimes inevitably occurs in the course of dealing with the tragedies of living. To be able to keep going and not lose hope, able to find humour in the absurdity of seemingly impossible situations. Nurturing our capacity for enthusiasm and excitement even though at times we fail. This book has been an effort to describe some of our strategies for survival.

REFERENCES AND BIBLIOGRAPHY

Anderson, H., & Goolishian, H. (1988). Human systems as linguistic systems: Preliminary and evolving ideas about implications for clinical theory. *Family Process, 27*, 371–393.

Anderson, H., & Goolishian, H. (1990). Beyond cybernetics: Comments on Atkinson and Heath's "Further thoughts on second-order family therapy." *Family Process, 29*, 157–163.

Bateson, G. (1972). *Steps to an Ecology of Mind.* New York: Jason Aronson.

Cecchin, G. (1987). Hypothesizing, circularity, and neutrality revisited: An invitation to curiosity. *Family Process, 26*, 405–413.

Cox, H. (1969). *The Feast of Fools.* New York: Harper.

De shazer, S. (1982). *Brief Ecosystemic Family Therapy.* New York: W.W. Norton.

Elkaim, M. (1990). *If You Love Me, Don't Love Me: Constructions of Reality and Change in Family Therapy.* New York: Basic Books.

Fromm-Reichmann, F. (1950). *Principles of Intensive Psychotherapy.* Chicago, IL: University of Chicago Press.

Gadamer, H. (1987). *Philosophical Hermeneutics.* Berkeley, CA: University of California Press.

Gergen, K. (1991). *The Saturated Self.* New York: Basic Books.

Goldner, V. (1988). Generation and gender: Normative and covert hierarchies. *Family Process, 27* (March), 17–31.

Haley, J. (1967). *Advanced Techniques of Hypnosis and Therapy: Selected Papers of Milton H. Erickson.* New York: Grune & Stratton.

Hoffman, L. (1990). A constructivist position for family therapy. *The Irish Journal of Psychotherapy, 1* (9), 110–129.

Hoopes, M., & Harper, J. (1987) *Birth Order and Sibling Patterns in Individual and Family Therapy.* Rockville, MD: Aspen.

Jackson, D., (1963). *The Sick, the Sad, the Savage, and the Sane.* Paper presented as the annual academic lecture to the Society of Medical Psychoanalysts and Department of Psychiatry, New York Medical College.

Keeney, B. (1983). *Aesthetics of Change.* New York: Guilford Press.

Keeney, B. (1982). Not pragmatic, not aesthetic. *Family Process,* 429–434.

Keeney, B., & Ross, J. (1985). *Mind in Therapy.* New York: Basic Books.

Laing, R. (1985). *Wisdom, Madness and Folly: The Making of a Psychiatrist.* New York: McGraw-Hill.

Lane, G., & Russell, T. (1987). Neutrality vs. social control: Systemic approach to violent couples. *Family Therapy Networker. 11* (3), 52–56.

Lane, G., & Schneider, A. (1990). A therapeutic ritual of respect. *Zeitschrift für Systemische Therapie, 8,* 103–108. Also in *Journal of Family Therapy, 12* (3), 287–294.

Maturana, H., & Varela, F. (1980). *Autopoiesis and Cognition: The Realization of the Living.* Dordrecht: D. Reidl.

Paglia, C. (1989). *Sexual Persona.* Cambridge, MA: Yale University Press.

Palazzoli, M., Boscolo, L., Cecchin, G., & Prata, G. (1978). *Paradox and Counterparadox.* New York: Jason Aronson.

Prigogine, L., & Stengers, I. (1984). *Order out of Chaos.* New York: Bantam.

Ray, W. (1991). The interactional therapy of Don D. Jackson. *Zeitschrift fur Systemische Therapie, 9,* 2–25.

Ray, W. (1992). Our future in the past: Lessons from Don D. Jackson for the practice of family therapy with hospitalized adolescents. *Family Therapy, 19* (1), 61–71.

Sluzki, C. (in press). *The "Better-Formed" Story.*

Sullivan, H.S. (1953). *The Collected Works of Harry Stack Sullivan.* New York: W.W. Norton.

Von Foerster, H. (1981) *Observing Systems*. Seaside, CA: Intersystems Publications.

Weakland, J. (1989). Personal interview with Wendel A. Ray. Palo Alto, CA: Mental Research Institute.

Webster's New Universal Unabridged Dictionary, 2nd ed. (1983). Cleveland, OH: Dorset & Berber.

Whitaker, C. (1976). The hindrance of theory in clinical work. In P. Guerin (Ed.), *Family Therapy: Theory and Practice* (pp. 154–164). New York: Gardner Press.

White, M. (1989). *Selected Papers*. Adelaide: Dulwich Centre.

ABOUT THE AUTHORS

Gianfranco Cecchin, M.D., is co-founder of Milan Systemic Therapy, one of the most influential family therapy models practised today. Co-Director of the Centro Milenese Di Terapia Della Famiglia, Milan, Italy, he is world renowned for his pioneering work in family therapy. He is author and co-author of numerous journal articles and books, including the classics *Paradox and Counterparadox* and *Milan Systemic Therapy*.

Gerry Lane, M.S.W., is in private practice and is the Director of Family Therapy at Hillside Hospital, Atlanta, Georgia. Author of a number of journal articles and book chapters, he has presented workshops throughout Europe and the United States. He has gained wide recognition for his pioneering use of cybernetic and systemic orientation in research and clinical practice with couples' violence. In recent years he has devoted much of his time expanding the use of the systemic orientation in psychiatric and other institutional settings.

Wendel A. Ray, Ph.D., is a Research Associate and Director of the Don D. Jackson Archive at the Mental Research Institute, Palo Alto, California. He is Co-Founder of The Family Therapy Institute of Louisiana, and an Associate Professor of Marriage and Family Therapy at Northeast Louisiana University in Monroe, Louisiana. An AAMFT Clinical member and supervisor, he is author of more than twenty-five journal articles and book chapters and has presented numerous workshops across the United States. He is President of the Louisiana Association for Marriage and Family Therapy.